Morticians Are Not Sentimentalists. The Questions They Asked Were of a Professional Nature . . .

But upon hearing that Marilyn had been dead for three hours, Guy Hockett, an owner of the Westwood Memorial Cemetery, gave his son a knowing look. His experience in these matters told him that Marilyn had been a corpse for longer than that.

Marilyn's body was stiff and, in order to strap it to the gurney, it had to be bent with some difficulty. Only a corpse in an advanced state of rigor mortis required such efforts. A body that had been dead for only three hours would have been much more supple and easier to handle.

Guy Hockett estimated that Marilyn had been dead approximately six to eight hours. That placed the time of her death at about 8:00 P.M., Saturday night, August 4th.

In the turmoil that followed, no one expressed doubts as to the manner of Marilyn's death . . . But as subsequent events revealed, the postmortem was staged for one purpose: to keep out the truth.

It was the beginning of the Marilyn Conspiracy.

THE MARILYN CONSPIRACY

MILO SPERIGLIO

PUBLISHED BY POCKET BOOKS NEW YORK

All insert photographs, unless otherwise indicated, are from the collection of Robert F. Slatzer.

Another *Original* publication of POCKET BOOKS

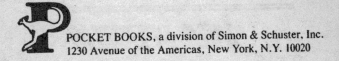

POCKET BOOKS, a division of Simon & Schuster, Inc.
1230 Avenue of the Americas, New York, N.Y. 10020

ISBN: 0-671-62612-4

First Pocket Books printing April, 1986

10 9 8 7 6 5 4 3 2 1

POCKET and colophon are registered trademarks
of Simon & Schuster, Inc.

Printed in the U.S.A.

FOREWORD

My name is Milo Speriglio. I am the director of Nick Harris Detectives in Los Angeles. Detectives are people who work with puzzles. For thirteen years, I've been working on a particularly intriguing puzzle. It concerns the death of Marilyn Monroe.

Some years ago I listened to a tape. It recorded a telephone conversation that took place sometime during the night of August 4, 1962. The call was placed from San Francisco to the home of Marilyn Monroe. The caller asked, "Is she dead yet?"

This was one piece of the puzzle. By the time I heard that tape, however, I already had a sufficient number of other pieces to fit it into the picture I was trying to assemble. I already knew, for instance, that there were three people inside Marilyn's home at the time the call was placed.

I also knew how the tape had come into existence. Marilyn's phone was being tapped on orders from Jimmy Hoffa, head of the Teamsters' Union. The person who had placed the tap was a legend in his field known as the "king of the wiretappers."

When a detective tries to unravel a crime, he begins at the beginning. He looks for motive.

5

What was Jimmy Hoffa's motive in wiring Marilyn's house?

It was not for the sake of the glamorous movie star. It was to "get the goods on Bobby Kennedy," the Attorney General, Marilyn's secret lover, and Hoffa's avowed enemy, who had publicly stated that he would put the union boss behind bars.

These are just a few of the pieces of the puzzle which will be put together in the following pages. Many of those "pieces" are now dead. Bobby and Jack Kennedy, their brother-in-law Peter Lawford, Jimmy Hoffa, the "king of the wiretappers," and assorted gangsters from the Las Vegas underworld—all except Lawford died a violent death or died under suspicious circumstances.

Other pieces of the puzzle which have helped me create the picture involve not people but documents, papers, official and unofficial, reports and tapes. By the time you have finished reading this book, the picture will be complete.

It will show beyond the shadow of a doubt that Marilyn Monroe did not commit suicide.

In the thirteen years I've spent tracking down clues to prove that Marilyn's death was not self-inflicted, one element has eluded me. It concerns a red diary which Marilyn kept during her affair with Bobby Kennedy.

In this intimate journal she makes references to, among other things, her affairs with Jack and Bobby Kennedy, her knowledge of the Bay of Pigs, the CIA plan to assassinate Fidel Castro through the use of gangsters, and various other matters of national interest.

Immediately after Marilyn's death, the diary was seen and read by several people. Then it mysteriously disappeared from the Coroner's office, along with other of her possessions that had been stored in a safe.

The disappearance of the red diary is only one element in the effort that has been going for nearly a quarter century to keep the true story of Marilyn's death from becoming public.

It's a conspiracy of silence that runs from the top government and law enforcement agencies to the people around Marilyn at the time of her death. The Marilyn Conspiracy still continues. Witness the repeated quashing of the demand by the Los Angeles County Board of Supervisors for a Grand Jury inquiry, and more recently the cancellation of the 1985 ABC TV-News 20/20 report on the death of Marilyn Monroe, which its own anchorpersons considered "better than anything the media had done since Watergate."

The recovery of the red diary is not the missing link that will prove her murder and point to her murderers. The red diary provides further insight into her relations with Bobby and Jack Kennedy, with Hollywood and Las Vegas, as well as a look into her own tortured psyche. It may also shed additional light on *why* she was murdered. This book already establishes that as fact. More important than Marilyn's diary are the clandestine tape recordings made in the Monroe home the night she died.

I hope that my findings will finally persuade a Grand Jury to convene and establish as a matter of record the circumstances of Marilyn Monroe's death and thereby close the sordid and tragic history of this case.

INTRODUCTION

In the beginning of the Marilyn Conspiracy there was a lifeless hand holding the telephone, the nude body sprawled across the bed, and the house on 12305 Helena Drive. Even though it's located in Brentwood, a high-priced neighborhood filled with quiet streets and luxuriant palms, the house is unassuming, a small one-story residence. No one would have guessed that its occupant was a famous movie star, perhaps *the* most famous star of the century. Other sirens of the screen like Jayne Mansfield, Zsa Zsa Gabor and Marion Davies had gone for pink castles and mansions built on the grand scale. Marilyn Monroe, for all her worldwide celebrity, felt most at ease with simplicity. She chose the house because she liked its Mexican motif, and it was just big enough to fill her needs.

After having lived for years in hotels, rented apartments and furnished houses, she had returned to Los Angeles to settle down. The house in Brentwood suited her. It was inconspicuous and it was in her home town. She had grown up and gone to school in the San Fernando Valley, just over the mountains. A few miles south was Hollywood, the geographical center of her world. At last, after the whirlwind years,

9

she had moved from the eye of the storm. She had a home in a city where she felt comfortable and familiar.

Inconspicuous and modest though it was, the house had features necessary to a star of her stature. A Spanish-style structure, it was just off Carmelina, a wide artery from which more than thirty Helena Drives extended like fingers north and south of Sunset Boulevard. All the Helena Drives were cul-de-sacs. Marilyn's house was at the very bottom of the street, making it impossible for rubberneckers to drive by for a glimpse of America's idol. To further protect her privacy it was surrounded by a high concrete wall and thick, forbidding wooden gates.

In 1961, after her divorce from playwright Arthur Miller, she wished to be done with depression, anxiety, and the physical ailments that had plagued her for years. She had a psychiatrist, Dr. Ralph Greenson, in whom she had implicit trust and whom she fully expected to help keep her emotional scales in balance. In Hyman Engelberg, an internist, she reposed a similar trust. She had a housekeeper, Mrs. Eunice Murray, recommended by Dr. Greenson, who besides taking care of the day-to-day tasks also served as a companion and live-in nurse. Another regular among her entourage was Norman Jeffries II, a handyman, the son-in-law of Mrs. Murray, who fixed things around the house. She had a press secretary, Pat Newcomb, whose job it was—more or less—to protect her. Included in the outer circle of retainers were a chauffeur, masseur, a hair stylist, PR man and makeup artist, all of whom she could rely on to be at her service at any hour of the day or night.

Apart from all these people, Marilyn had friends whom she felt loved her and had her interests at heart.

There were Paula and Lee Strasberg, who jointly acted as her dramatic coach and mentor; they had inspired her to shed her sex symbol image, assuring her that she had talent to become a serious film artist. Though she rarely availed herself of them, she had carte blanche entree to the biggest names in Hollywood, from studio moguls to the most famous stars. In fact, her friends spanned the range of *Who's Who* in American entertainment, social life and politics. She could pick up the phone and call Frank Sinatra or another member of the "Rat Pack," Peter Lawford. She could call the White House, and her call would be passed on to the President or the Attorney General without delay.

So when Marilyn Monroe purchased the house in late 1961, everything pointed to the stabilization of a life that from birth had pitched and rolled like a stricken vessel. It was the first house she had ever owned. She stocked the closets with a whole new wardrobe from Saks Fifth Avenue and Jaks of Beverly Hills. To buy a house without a husband or children made her feel lonely. Yet, she'd been happy too. But just six months after she bought it, the house in which Marilyn Monroe had invested her hopes for happiness became her tomb. She took her last breath in its master bedroom. For many hours through the night of August 4 and into the following morning, her nude body lay cold and lifeless, sprawled across her bed.

In the early hours of August 5, 1962, the weekend Watch Commander at the West Los Angeles Police Station was Sgt. Jack Clemmons, a burly officer who wore black-framed glasses. Although he often wore a quizzical expression, he always acted in a direct, forthright manner. Normally, the weekend watch was quiet, free from the hubbub that filled the halls during the week.

Clemmons was drinking coffee and doing routine paperwork when the phone rang. He picked up the receiver and heard someone identify himself as Dr. Hyman Engelberg. In a voice whose calm seemed the result of extreme self-control, the caller reported the death of a 36-year-old woman by the name of Marilyn Monroe.

Sgt. Clemmons looked at his watch. It was 4:35 A.M. Hurriedly, he wrote down the address, and after appointing another officer to take his place, he rushed off in his squad car in the direction of Sunset Boulevard.

On his way, he radioed for a second squad car to meet him at 12305 Helena Drive for assistance. As an experienced cop, Clemmons knew that many news reporters had car radios tuned in to the police band. He could picture them coursing through the darkened streets like hounds in pursuit of prey. He had to get there before the quiet Brentwood neighborhood filled with a crush of cars and a clamoring media mob. If any reporter had been dozing, Clemmons's transmission over the police band would have awakened him like a bombshell.

Clemmons pulled up before the massive wooden gates at Marilyn's home. He noticed three cars parked in the driveway. A prim, well-kept lady opened the door. She introduced herself as the housekeeper, Mrs. Eunice Murray. With a nod, she confirmed the policeman's query that Marilyn Monroe was dead. She said she had discovered the body shortly after midnight, after having observed light coming from under Marilyn's door.

"Who else is here?" Clemmons asked.

"Two doctors," Mrs. Murray answered. "Dr. Greenson, Marilyn's psychiatrist, and Dr. Engelberg, her internist."

Clemmons asked how long the doctors had been there. The housekeeper said they'd been with Marilyn since 12:30 A.M. Clemmons had received Dr. Engelberg's call at 4:35 A.M. That meant that Marilyn had been dead for approximately three to four hours. The police sergeant thought it odd that the doctors had waited so long to notify the authorities.

After being led into Marilyn's bedroom, Clemmons saw the two doctors seated on chairs beside the body, which was spread diagonally across the bed, covered with a sheet. Dr. Ralph Greenson, the psychiatrist, had his head in his hands. When Clemmons entered, he didn't look up but kept his eyes fixed on the floor. When, after a few minutes, he raised his head, Clemmons was startled to see that the psychiatrist "had a smirk on his face and didn't look natural."

Dr. Engelberg, like his colleague, was well-dressed, his light wavy hair carefully coiffed—he looked like a doctor in a television drama. But the policeman noticed he seemed crestfallen. Clemmons thought he looked "remorseful." The housekeeper looked "scared."

The eyes of both men followed him as he gently drew back the sheet that covered the body. The face known to millions of moviegoers all over the globe was indeed that of Marilyn Monroe. She was lying face down, without makeup, her lustrous blond hair spread out like a halo. A telephone cord ran over one side of the bed and lay beneath her. The dead woman's right arm was outstretched as if reaching for the phone. Dr.

Greenson had found the phone in her lifeless hand and had removed it, according to his initial report to the police.

Like every newspaper reader, Clemmons was familiar with the drama of Marilyn's life and career: a father who had left before she was born; a mother who had shuttled in and out of mental institutions; a young, bewildered girl by the name of Norma Jeane shifting between foster homes; a runaway who never completed high school; the stunning woman-on-the-make who finally "made" it; and now sadly, the dead body, more famous in death than it had been in life. Marilyn's immense appeal as a movie star had always been a mixture of raw sensuality and childlike innocence. The sensuality had fled from her blue, rigid form; only the soft, childlike innocence remained.

When Sgt. Clemmons came to Marilyn's house, he had already been informed that her death was a suicide. The doctors had quietly pointed to the fifteen bottles of over-the-counter and prescription medicines that cluttered her nightstand. The policeman's attention was particularly drawn to one bottle lying on its side, its cap a few inches away. The label listed the name of the pharmacist, the prescription number, and its contents: Nembutal.

Dr. Engelberg mentioned that he had approved a prescription refill of the drug two days before, and that it had contained fifty capsules. The obvious inference was that Marilyn, after taking this lethal dosage earlier in the evening, had quietly expired.

The police sergeant was neither a forensic expert nor was it his job to play Columbo. He was a law enforcement professional whose duty it was to establish the facts, record the information and enter these on his report. It would be up to others—experts in their respective fields, higher-ups with full investigative powers—to complete the process he had initiated. But from the very moment he entered the master bedroom, the first hint of suspicion lodged itself in his mind.

One of the first questions he posed was why the two doctors present had waited so long before notifying the police. Their answers had been evasive. Of course, the doctors were protected by the rules of professional confidentiality. Furthermore, without a formal charge, they were under no compulsion to answer *any* question. But their responses—a shrugging of the shoulders and a mumbled "we were just talking"—had struck the officer as being, under the circumstances, unusually casual.

"About what?" Clemmons asked. "What were you talking about?"

The doctors stared at him blankly without speaking.

As he let his eyes roam over the bedroom, Clemmons became more suspicious. He noted that Mrs. Murray, the housekeeper, seemed driven by an exaggerated sense of orderliness. The officer watched as she moved unobtrusively—"as if she were walking on eggshells," Clemmons recalls—from one room to another. He saw her clear out the refrigerator and dump its contents. He saw her load boxes into her car, while at the same time the washing machine and dryer monotonously hummed, breaking the silence of the house. With proper respect for her diligence, Clemmons could not refrain from asking why she was doing the laundry at five in the morning while her employer lay dead in the bedroom.

Unruffled and rather abrupt, she replied that it was her understanding that the Coroner would soon be sealing off the house. She was merely making sure that everything was clean and tidy.

Clemmons supposed that this process had already been in swing long before he arrived. The bedroom in which Marilyn lay lifeless displayed a neat configuration of objects. The bathroom off her bedroom showed an orderly arrangement of toiletries and towels as would befit a well-run home. In the bedroom itself, a few handwoven "cobra" baskets were placed along one wall. A pile of clothes, meticulously folded, together with a stack of purses, stood against the far wall. The pill bottles on the nightstand, apart from the empty Nembutal bottle lying on its side, seemed to have been set up by a methodical hand. The only sign of disorder showed itself in the bedcovers, which were bunched about the beige comforter.

For the police sergeant, this was not the first time he had been summoned to a room in which the victim had died of an overdose of sleeping capsules. Marilyn's room, however, was the first he had found in such remarkable order. Contrary to the common conception that an overdose of sleeping pills is an easy and painless way to die, in some cases the victim suffers an agonizingly convulsive death. In the final moments before losing consciousness, the victim often suffers terrible choking gasps accompanied by vomiting and uncoordinated movements. This frequently results in stumbling over furniture, knocking things about, scattering and breaking fragile objects. Sgt. Clemmons saw no evidence of any of this, evidence which experience had taught him was common in overdose cases.

While noting these discrepancies, Clemmons became even more intrigued by the absence of that one item without which fifty capsules of Nembutal could not have been swallowed. Neither the nightstand nor the floor, nor any other place in the bedroom, revealed a drinking glass or cup. Even more curiously, the bathroom just then was being remodeled; its plumbing did not work, so no water could be had from its faucets. Clemmons wondered whether the doctors had not been similarly struck by the absence of a drinking glass or the lack of ready availability of water. But he was not there to fish for information. His job was limited, to observe and record what he saw.

Clemmons could not help feeling, though, as he went about his duties, that there was more here than met the eye. He wondered how the doctors could state with such apparent assurance that the cause of death had been suicide. As medical professionals, they should have had at least the discretion to wait until the Coroner had done his work before making their pronouncement. Only an autopsy would reveal the cause of death. Sgt. Clemmons had the distinct impression that the doctors were hiding something.

His suspicions increased when he examined Marilyn's body. Death had set its seal on the skin with a deep purple coloring. The process called lividity—the settling of blood—follows the stage of discoloration which first turns the skin ashen-gray. Clemmons knew that lividity indicates in what position the person died, since blood always seeks the lowest level. He also knew that this process takes considerable time. The purple flush was spread throughout Marilyn's posterior from head to toe. He assumed, therefore, that she had died not on her stomach, as he had found her, but on her back.

But more significant in strengthening his doubts as to how long Marilyn had been dead was her body's extreme state of rigidity. Her advanced state of rigor mortis indicated that she must have been dead much longer than the three hours suggested by the doctors. For a condition of rigidity such as he observed, four to six hours should have passed. Clemmons now believed that Marilyn had taken her last breath sometime between 8:00 and 9:00 P.M. on August 4th—the previous night—not merely three hours earlier, as the doctors had suggested.

"It looked like the whole thing had been staged," Sgt. Clemmons said afterward while describing the death scene. "She couldn't have died in that position—face down, stretched out swanlike. To me, it was an out-and-out case of murder."

The policeman's last duty that morning was to call and break the tragic news to James Dougherty, a friend of his and a fellow police officer in Van Nuys.

Dougherty had been Marilyn's first husband. She had married him at sixteen, choosing marriage instead of placement in another foster home. Like all the men in Marilyn's life, Dougherty was never able to forget her. Upon his retirement, he withdrew with the memory of his child bride to a small town in Maine.

In a few brief words, Clemmons told his colleague that his former wife was dead.

"I was expecting it," Dougherty said after a pause.

Clemmons did not tell him what he really suspected; that Marilyn was not a suicide but a murder victim.

By the time Sgt. Clemmons went off duty, the whole Los Angeles press corps seemed to be milling in the street. They were joined by neighbors and curious onlookers. Quiet Helena Drive had turned into bedlam. It was as if a calamity had struck. No news, unless it concerned the death of a president, an earthquake, or a declaration of war, could have brought about a like frenzy.

Sgt. Clemmons was relieved by Sgt. Robert Byron, who continued the investigation. Meanwhile, Mrs. Murray's obsessive housecleaning continued unabated. One thing especially appeared to have bothered her, and she called her son-in-law, Norman Jeffries, to take care of it. There was a broken window in Marilyn's bedroom. Jeffries was urged to come over immediately and repair it. He succeeded in doing so before the police photographers arrived on the scene.

The next visitors to the house were Guy Hockett and his son, Don. Guy Hockett was one of the owners of the Westwood Memorial Cemetery. Hockett was the local Coroner's representative assigned to Marilyn's area during the month of August. Each month, under a rotation system, the L.A. County Coroner's office used a different mortuary to serve the outlying parts of the city. In the early morning hours of Saturday, August 5, Guy Hockett had received the stunning call to pick up Marilyn's corpse.

The Hocketts arrived on the scene in a nondescript white van intended to minimize drawing attention to their presence. They managed to pass through the barred gate, entered the driveway, and backed the van up to the front door. Upon entering Marilyn's bedroom, they ordered everyone else out of the room. Father and son first collected the pill bottles, establishing that there were fifteen. This was part of their duty in assisting the L.A. County Coroner's office, which was charged with making the official report.

Morticians are not sentimentalists. The fact that America's reigning movie queen required their expertise did not prevent them from carrying out their task with dispatch. The questions they asked were of a professional nature. But upon hearing that Marilyn had been dead for three hours, Guy Hockett gave his son a knowing look. Like Sgt. Clemmons before him, his experience in these matters told him that Marilyn had been a corpse for longer than that.

They arrived at the same conclusion that Clemmons did. The body was "stiff" and in order to strap it to the gurney it had to be "bent" with some difficulty. Only a corpse in an advanced state of rigor mortis required such efforts. A body that had been dead for only three hours would have been much more supple and easier to handle.

Independent of Sgt. Clemmons, Guy and Don Hockett estimated that Marilyn had been dead approximately six to eight hours. That placed the time of her death at about 8:00 P.M., Saturday night, August 4th.

In the turmoil that followed, no one expressed doubts as to the manner of Marilyn's death or offered the same observations as Clemmons and Hockett. But as subsequent events revealed, the postmortem was staged for one purpose: to keep out the truth.

It was the beginning of the Marilyn Conspiracy.

THE MARILYN CONSPIRACY

Chapter One

THE CASE

"Marilyn Monroe did not kill herself. She was killed. I've got a man here who can prove that she did not commit suicide."

My efforts to uncover the Marilyn Conspiracy began thirteen years ago. Today I can look back at the death scene in the early morning hours of August 5, 1962, and commend Sgt. Clemmons for immediately "smelling a rat." After logging thousands of hours, talking to hundreds of people, and poring over sheafs of documents, I can reconstruct a death scene which neither the police officer at the time, nor anyone else for that matter, could have pictured in their wildest imaginations.

The routine suicide to which the sergeant had been called, the orderliness of the house, the telltale Nembutal bottle, the subsequent autopsy, the official report of Marilyn's death—all were fictions that have been maintained for over two decades. For some time the cover-up was successful—a death certificate was fudged, the autopsy report was altered and reconstructed, evidence was destroyed and changed, crucial items of Marilyn's property disappeared, her telephone records vanished, no inquest was held, and those with knowledge of the true state of affairs were never questioned under oath.

Before I begin to unravel the Marilyn Conspiracy, I will first establish the sequence of certain events preceding the hour of Marilyn's death. These points will be developed more fully in subsequent chapters. They are all based on fact, witnesses, and evidence I myself and others associated with me have uncovered. I mention them now so that I will be better able to describe the events that lead to one inescapable conclusion. There was a cover-up:

• Marilyn did not commit suicide. An empty Nembutal bottle was placed on her nightstand before the police arrived. According to the original Coroner's report no traces of Nembutal were found in her gastric contents. This means that she did not take them orally. Marilyn died as the result of a fatal injection by the hands of others.

• The original body diagrams showed bruises on Marilyn's body, both front and back. Subsequently, these bruises were neither shown nor mentioned. This leads to the conclusion that a struggle took place, possibly as the result on her part of resisting the hypodermic needle or syringe that was being administered.

• Marilyn did not die at home in her bed, as stated in the official report. Sometime in the early morning of August 5, an ambulance from Schaefer Ambulance Service was dispatched to Marilyn's home. The medical attendants found her comatose and rushed her to the Santa Monica Hospital. According to Walter

Schaefer, president of the company, "Marilyn expired at the hospital."

• Someone, or more than one person, managed to take Marilyn's dead body from the hospital. She was returned to her home. Her clothes were removed and her nude body was spread in an anterior position diagonally across the bed.

• Mrs. Murray, Marilyn's housekeeper, did not discover her dead body shortly after midnight, as she stated to Sgt. Clemmons. She now confirms that she did not make this discovery until about 3:30 A.M. Nor was it the light coming from under her door that originally attracted her attention. She has gone on record that the "telephone cord" led her to Marilyn's bedroom.

• Bobby Kennedy, Peter Lawford and a doctor with a "medical bag" were with Marilyn on the last day of her life. Neighbors saw Bobby Kennedy enter her house. Mrs. Murray, after years of silence, has now gone on record: "Yes, the ambulance took Marilyn . . . Bobby Kennedy was at the house."

• Peter Lawford, the actor, the Kennedys' brother-in-law, played a vital role in the circumstances surrounding Marilyn's demise. He went to her house after her death to "clean things up"; that is, to remove all traces of Bobby Kennedy's earlier presence. He also sent in "Mr. O," a noted Hollywood private eye, to dispose of anything he, Lawford, might have missed. Lawford also helped Bobby Kennedy get out of town during that night and helped "clean things up" after a lovers' quarrel.

Marilyn Monroe died like a bystander who gets caught in the "cross fire" between two opposing forces. She became involved with dangerous people. Naively, she stumbled into secret domains. She knew too much. A man had scorned her. She was about to tell all. Then she died.

As chief detective of the world's second oldest agency, it's my business to "know" a lot of people. My office cabinet bulges with the names of people in all walks of life whom I can call upon for assistance. Many of my contacts are honest, upright men and women holding responsible positions in the world of business and government. Some are on the shady side, but their inside knowledge in somewhat dubious fields often dictates that I cultivate them.

Among my favorite contacts, and the ones I find most reliable and congenial, are newspaper people, especially investigative reporters. I regard them as brothers-under-the-skin. There is an affinity among us, a natural rapport which stems from our common interest in getting the facts and uncovering the truth. I've often worked side by side with them on cases, and many of them have become close friends. I've helped them, and on more than one occasion I've been grateful for leads they've provided me.

I was not surprised, therefore, to receive a call from my old friend Al Stump in September 1972. Al has since retired, but at the time he was an investigative reporter for the *Herald Examiner*. He was a rumpled, skeptical, dyed-in-the-wool journalist of the old stamp, a fountain of stories and anecdotes which, I'm afraid, are unsuitable for print. In my book, he was one of the best, most thorough and most reliable reporters in the business.

"Milo," I heard his brisk, gruff voice ask, "got a moment?"

"Sure, Al. Shoot."

Al Stump was not a man to call simply in order to chat. It had to be important.

"Are you sitting down?" he asked.

I told him I was.

"Marilyn Monroe was murdered!"

For a second I held my breath.

"You're kidding . . ." I gasped.

"Marilyn Monroe did *not* kill herself," Al said emphatically. *"She was killed.* I've got a man here who can prove that she did not commit suicide."

My mind raced back to 1962, when I, like the rest of the world, had been shocked by the report of her death. I couldn't help taking it personally when I'd first heard the newscast. After all, she'd been America's sweetheart, the queen of the screen, who lived her life publicly with all its ups and downs. But since then, though I had read the newspaper articles and some of the books about her, I can't say that she'd remained in the forefront of my mind. Life goes on. Marilyn Monroe was for me a legend, like Jean Harlow or Clara Bow, someone whose sex appeal and allure had captured the national imagination, but who was now a figure rooted in the past.

But Al Stump rekindled my curiosity. When a respected investigative reporter for a major newspaper calls and makes an outright declaration that what everybody had believed all these years was wrong, he must have solid reasons. He must be taken seriously.

"Look, Al," I said, "what are you telling me? Everybody knows Marilyn took her own life."

"Milo," Al said, "I want you to meet a person I've got with me here. He can tell you a story that'll make your hair stand on end. He needs your help. The guy's received threats on his life. He's scared, and I don't blame him. I would be, too. With the information he's got, he's walking around with a time bomb."

I protested weakly, "Al, I'm a very busy man. I haven't got time to fool around."

Al, who knew me well enough, took this to mean, "OK, we're coming over." The meeting was set for the same afternoon at my Wilshire Boulevard office.

When I hung up, I hadn't the foggiest notion that I would soon be involved in the "crime of the century." Nor could I have imagined that a decade later, on August 4, 1982—the twentieth anniversary of Marilyn's death—I would mount the rostrum at the Greater Los Angeles Press Club and startle the packed house with the announcement: "Marilyn Monroe was murdered . . ."

Al Stump entered my office together with a stocky, conservatively dressed man in his early forties carrying a briefcase. Those who practice my profession set great store on first impressions. We don't always trust our intuition, but I've often found out that I should have gone with my initial feeling. The man accompanying Al struck me as immediately sympathetic. He had an outward calm. Beneath it, though, I sensed a great deal of tension.

I decided there and then that I'd accept him as a client. I had no inkling, of course, that I had just committed myself to taking on the longest-running case in the agency's seventy-five-year history.

Professional people, whether they are bureaucrats, doctors, lawyers or newspapermen, usually manage to maintain some distance between themselves and the cases or problems they deal with. As a detective, I share that attitude; without it, our lives would be in ceaseless turmoil. But what struck me about my "confidant" was that despite the decade that had passed, he was still as emotionally involved—almost obsessed—by the question of Marilyn's death as if it had happened yesterday. I soon learned why.

He had been in love with Marilyn since both were in their early twenties and living on the fringes of Hollywood. Marilyn was then an aspiring starlet, and he was a cub newspaper reporter, fresh from the Midwest, hoping to break into screen writing and directing. They shared a brief romance, carefree and happy-go-lucky on the part of Marilyn, intense and serious on the part of the young writer. Sheepishly, though with a bittersweet pride, my confidant admitted that they'd actually been married.

In my business, I run into every type of "flake" making the most outlandish allegations. I must have looked skeptical, because Al began to nod between puffs at his pipe, as if to say, "Listen to him, Milo, the guy's for real."

"Actually, it was sort of a lark," the man admitted. "We got married for five days in Mexico in August of 1952. We spent our wedding night at the Rosarita Beach Hotel. We had a witness by the name of Noble Chissell. After we got back, we quietly destroyed the marriage license because at that time marriage just didn't fit into her plans. Marilyn wasn't looking for an ideal husband. Her career was just taking off, and she wasn't interested in a house with a white fence and kids romping in the backyard."

After that admission, we got down to business. He opened his briefcase and began the story that explained why he believed Marilyn had been murdered. He had been conducting his own investigation for the past ten years and had completed a manuscript. As a result, his life had been threatened; his publisher had already been subjected to physical violence and warned not to proceed with publication.

Within five minutes, I was spellbound. I signaled my secretary to hold my calls and to tell all visitors that I was unavailable for the rest of the afternoon.

"You've got to remember," my confidant began, "that Marilyn Monroe never felt she was Hollywood's 'Golden Girl.' Marilyn was basically always Norma Jeane, a sweet, spontaneous, softhearted and gentle American girl who wouldn't hurt a fly. The world saw her as a sex goddess. She was getting 20,000 fan letters a week, some of them from multimillionaires proposing marriage. It always puzzled her, but she liked the attention she was getting from men, especially powerful men. Frank Sinatra was one of her lovers. So was Jack Kennedy who, after he was through with her, passed her on to his brother. She had twelve abortions. She wasn't sure whether the last one's father was Jack or Bobby. She was basically innocent and trusting. Her tragedy was that she got in over her head."

Years later, I would discover just what my confidant had meant by that phrase, "in over her head." The pleasant, secluded house in which she died was "wired" from top to bottom. Everything that took place within the confines of her walls was tapped, taped, bugged and recorded. Every word she or anyone with her uttered would find itself transposed onto tapes. They even listened in her bathroom. Some of the most advanced bugging apparatus of its time— such as the voice-activated recorder—was operating in her home.

The real pathos in all this eavesdropping, as I learned soon after entering the investigation, was not its focus on Marilyn because of her stardom. She was merely a chip in a high-stakes game involving the White House, the FBI, the CIA, the nation's most powerful union boss and members of the Mafia. Her house was rigged with electronic devices to "set up" the Kennedys, particularly Bobby. Marilyn Monroe, the "chip" in the game, could be discarded the moment she was no longer "negotiable."

My confidant's name was Bob Slatzer. He was born in Ohio, and had been a reporter for Midwest newspapers before establishing himself as a writer-director-producer in Hollywood. At the time I met him, he was 45 years old. Since Marilyn's death, he had been conducting his own private investigation, using his own funds. Now, ten years later, he confessed that it was beyond his strength. He needed professional help. He'd begun to feel paranoid. He knew there were people "out there" who took a dim view of what he was doing.

With Al Stump sitting by, I listened to Bob Slatzer for over three hours on that smoggy afternoon in September 1972. When he was done I asked him, "Have you ever been polygraphed before?"

He said no, but that he had no objection to submitting to one. Using a voice-stress polygraph unit, I hooked him up, and for the next 20 minutes I fired questions. The voice-stress unit never departed from its normal levels. He came out "positive" in every respect.

That same week, I submitted a proposal to the board of directors of my agency to commence a full-scale investigation into the death of Marilyn Monroe. I submitted that my client, Bob Slatzer, had neither the means, the expertise, nor the time to continue his own investigation. The board agreed to pay the investigation costs, with the condition that the Marilyn case would not interfere with my regular fee-paying assignments. I agreed to this condition, not knowing that from then on every minute of my spare time would be devoted to following the trail which Bob provided for me.

Bob Slatzer had a number of documents and affidavits that bore out the Marilyn Conspiracy in rough detail. But in order to conclusively prove murder we needed more evidence—evidence that could stand up to the most minute analysis in order to place the matter beyond a reasonable doubt.

I narrowed down the areas in which to conduct our search to six: the L.A. County Coroner's office, the L.A. Police Department, the FBI/CIA complex, friends and confidants of Marilyn, the Jimmy Hoffa/ Las Vegas circle, and the Kennedy clan. My odyssey took ten years.

In the course of my investigation, it was inevitable that I would be approached by publicity-seekers, sensationalists, and charlatans. It was equally unavoidable that I would be inundated with spicy samples of Marilyn's love life. Some of these I cannot describe by any term other than "sick." For example, an employee of the morgue alleged that certain people had intercourse with Marilyn's corpse. Others were just humorous. For instance, the time in 1954 when Frank Sinatra and Marilyn's former husband Joe DiMaggio, along with private investigator Freddy Otash—"Mr. O"—intent on finding Marilyn in bed with a lover, went crashing into her neighbor's apartment. I have this item filed under W, "Wrong Door."

Marilyn's sex life, however, except as it bore on my efforts to uncover the Marilyn Conspiracy, held no interest for me. What concerned me in exposing the cover-up were the roles of the L.A. Police Department, the work of the "king of the wiretappers," the Coroner's and toxicology reports, the people involved in the autopsy, the private files of L.A.'s Chief of Detectives, the record of Bobby Kennedy's whereabouts on the fatal day of Marilyn's death, the items of her property that had disappeared, the FBI files on Marilyn, and a slew of other puzzling information concerning her death.

My prime objective in exposing the Marilyn Conspiracy was to stimulate the L.A. County Board of Supervisors and the District Attorney's office into opening an investigation. Ten years later, I felt sufficiently convinced to demand a formal inquest into Marilyn's death by the Grand Jury. My findings proved "murder," which was the legal requirement to justify the appointment of a Grand Jury. Otherwise, under the law, any impropriety that was involved in any cover-up, whether proved or not, could not be prosecuted because of the expiration date of the Statute of Limitations.

This would apply to anything that took place the night Marilyn died—except *murder,* for which there is no Statute of Limitations.

When you launch a criminal investigation of this sort, you begin by stumbling in the dark. Fortunately, thanks to Bob Slatzer's work, I had my parameters already roughly defined. Nevertheless, it's always useful to have a starting point at which the motives of the protagonists and the events connect to provide lines of orientation. I located that point on the day of August 6, 1962.

Marilyn had scheduled a press conference on that day, during which she planned to reveal her intimate relations with Bobby and Jack Kennedy. To her confidants she had promised that at this meeting with the press she would tell all—her abortion, her knowledge of national security matters, her fears for her life, and the cavalier treatment she had suffered at the hands of Bobby.

If Marilyn had "told all" at that news conference, the consequences would have been incalculable. Her top-secret revelations could have caused a furor greater than the Teapot Dome scandal. It could have been as devastating as Watergate. It could have sparked an explosive situation with Cuba and the Soviet Union. John Kennedy, not Richard Nixon, might have become the first U.S. president to resign from office. The aspirations of Bobby Kennedy to succeed his brother would have been shattered.

But the press conference never took place.

The day before it was scheduled, Marilyn Monroe died.

Chapter Two

THE DIARY

Bobby told me today, "I want to put that S.O.B. Jimmy Hoffa into jail, no matter how I do it!"

During the last week of her life, Marilyn told several people that if she did not hear from Bobby Kennedy, she was going to blow the lid "off this whole damn thing." When Bob Slatzer heard about this, he talked to her long-distance on the evening of August 3, 1962, the day before she died, from Columbus, Ohio. Bob is a wildlife buff, and he was on location in Ohio for a nature film he was producing.

"What do you mean about 'blowing the lid off'?" he asked.

Marilyn announced that in a few days she was going to hold a news conference at which she would reveal the contents of her diary. She was going to get even with Bobby. She felt he had cruelly "used" her.

Sometime earlier Marilyn had confided to my client that she thought someone was listening to her telephone calls. It was not her first experience with eavesdroppers. There'd been "tails," gumshoes, hidden mikes and clandestine recorders after her divorce from America's baseball hero, Joe DiMaggio. Joe had been jealous. The "Wrong Door Raid" had given Hollywood something to chuckle over for weeks.

But in the final days of her life, it was not a possessive male that she feared. She couldn't put her finger precisely on who she thought was bugging her. She had a feeling, though, that if her phone was tapped, it had to have something to do with Bobby.

Her way of dealing with threatening situations was always to disregard them. In her own charmed life, the perils she ignored somehow had always redounded to advantage. But this time, her fears made her paranoid. For the more "sensitive" calls, she used pay phones in the neighborhood. She began carrying a heavy bag of coins. She called Slatzer from a phone booth that evening before her death, because she wanted to know more about Bobby's coming to California.

The day before, Slatzer had telephoned Marilyn with the news that Robert Kennedy was going to be in San Francisco that weekend to address the American Bar Association. He hadn't really wanted to tell her; he'd rather, so to speak, let sleeping dogs lie. But the dogs already were awake, baying to be heard. Marilyn had her fixation, her obsession, and Slatzer thought that by telling her, she would perhaps be able to get hold of Bobby, and possibly settle the matter. As he rang off, he asked her to let him know whether she'd been able to work it out.

Marilyn called back the next day. She sounded upset. She'd tried to reach Bobby Kennedy at the Justice Department in Washington two days running, and it looked like he was still avoiding her. She said she was going to find out where he'd be staying in San Francisco.

Though Slatzer had known Marilyn for close to two decades, and knew all about her habit of sleepwalking through danger, what he now heard worried him. Perhaps her innocence had always protected her, but now he felt she was playing with fire. He'd always looked askance at her affair with the president's brother. He suspected that for this cocky Kennedy, Marilyn was merely a beautiful toy, a rare brand name in sex, like Gucci in leather or Rolls-Royce in cars. He warned her of the consequences. He pleaded that to "expose" the President and Attorney General was folly.

Unperturbed by these misgivings voiced by her friend, Marilyn recalled that Bobby's sister Pat, Peter Lawford's wife, might know where in San Francisco her brother might be staying. Brightly, she suggested she'd call the Lawfords in Santa Monica to find out. Slatzer made another attempt to keep her from her mad pursuit. But adamantly Marilyn repeated, "If he keeps avoiding me, I might just call a press conference and tell them about it."

Three weeks earlier, Marilyn had shown Slatzer the diary: paging through it, he'd felt a chill. The entries he saw were compromising in the extreme. If she went ahead with the press conference, she might be giving away state secrets. That involved even greater danger to herself than merely exposing her affairs with the Kennedy brothers and creating a scandal. He pointed this out to her.

"I can care less," Marilyn said.

"And what about your diary?" Slatzer asked.

"It's safe," she replied. "Now, since my file cabinet

has been broken into twice, I keep it in one of my big purses all the time."

Slatzer tried to make her see that purse or no purse, she was walking around with a "time bomb."

Then he heard a laugh, fragile, without merriment. The sound had a sharpness, a jagged edge, as of breaking glass.

"It just might explode in the wrong faces," she said.

Less than twenty-four hours later, the little red diary did "explode," though not, as Marilyn had ingenuously hoped, in the "wrong faces."

When I first heard about Marilyn's red diary, I felt disinclined to believe in its existence. Skepticism is the detective's occupational frame of mind. I began by asking why Marilyn should want to keep a diary.

Today, as I look back, after thirteen years of studying Marilyn Monroe, I feel I know her as well as the palm of my hand. But when I first undertook the investigation into her death, Marilyn to me was still very much a cardboard figure. I saw the surface, the gloss, the pose, America's Venus, the magnificent blonde, the striking face, the extraordinary body tooled like a racing car. When I started out by asking why she kept a diary, it showed that I had as yet little understanding of her person.

My new client gave me my first inkling of Marilyn's complicated psyche. She came from a poor background, with an unstable mother, Gladys Monroe Mortenson, who was periodically away in a mental home and who had been married twice. The name of Gladys's first husband, John N. Baker, was used by Norma Jeane into her early teens, but when she first came to Hollywood she went back to using Norma Jeane Mortenson. Her mother's second husband,

Marilyn's father, had been Martin G. Mortenson, a Norwegian immigrant who left his wife and daughter three months after Norma Jeane was born in the Los Angeles County Hospital. According to Bob Slatzer, who has traced Martin Mortenson through the Chicago archives, he died in that city a few years later as the result of an accident in the work yard.

Before she married at sixteen, Norma Jeane lived in a dozen foster homes. I soon learned that in order to understand Marilyn and the web of intrigue woven round her final months, I had to forget about the cardboard cutout or the American Venus. I had to always bear in mind that I was dealing not with Marilyn Monroe but with Norma Jeane, the girl from the wrong side of the tracks, who, being an orphan, feeling rejected and unwanted, suffered the most crushing fate that can befall a child.

All the people I talked to who knew Marilyn spoke of the legacy of Norma Jeane's loveless early years. In later years, when Marilyn Monroe became a star, the personality that came through from behind the glittering mask was one marked by crushing insecurity. At the studios, with the cameras rolling, it became her notorious "stage fright," leading to production delays of almost every film in which she worked. The studio publicity chose to portray this as an endearing "shyness." Her insecurity made for that mix of waif and whore which was her great attraction for older men. Younger men responded to the sheer animal sexuality. She was a woman for all men, a general male fantasy. Women envied her and empathized with her. But even few of her closest friends could say they knew her. The public certainly did not know her, nor did Marilyn know herself.

As a public sex symbol the whole world was her

stage, but the fright never left her. Abandoning school in the tenth grade, her education had continued on the Hollywood streets, and all her life Marilyn painfully felt the lack of cultural attainment. People who did not sense the emptiness she often felt came away describing her as a "zombie," an "underwater creature with glassy eyes"; "impossible to get through to," they said, not realizing that they'd come away not from Marilyn Monroe but from scared, bewildered Norma Jeane.

But this insecure girl, who was "shy" because she felt out of place everywhere, became that quintessential American phenomenon—a "celebrity." Before she died, Marilyn inhabited the pantheon reserved for America's entertainment idols. She became a screen star, a public divinity, an American goddess.

Marilyn Monroe worked extraordinarily hard to reach the immense goal she set herself. Her beauty alone, her charm, the "electricity," or the fact that she used her body to advance herself, do not explain her astonishing career. What accounts for Marilyn's success was the iron determination to "make" it, to live down the legacy of Norma Jeane, which included a history of madness on both sides of the family.

Her mother, who'd been employed in the studios as a film cutter, named her after Norma Talmadge, the Thirties' famed screen star. As a child, Marilyn used to dream that Clark Gable was her father. She felt herself destined, and her velvety flesh concealed a formidable will. It was steeled during her scramble upward. It helped transform her into an accomplished actress, a screen goddess and box-office hit. And that same weapon which had helped her triumph over Hollywood she wielded in her drive to make up for the pedigree, the background, the family, the "finish" Norma Jeane had gone without.

Marilyn's friends and acquaintances were always surprised when they saw her take notes. An opinion, a witticism or joke, an item of information, a discriminating taste, words which she thought wise coming from the mouth of someone she respected would often be transcribed into a little notebook. It had been a habit from the time success first thrust her into the company of prominent men. While married to playwright Arthur Miller, she learned to love being around artists, poets, writers and intellectuals. Their talk provided quick remedies to filling the gaps. She imagined that once the vacuum was full, her inner shape would take on firmness. She suffered from being "Marilyn," a sex symbol that deprived her of real identity. She was always eager to have books or works of art explained to her. Hating the idea of the "dumb blonde," she made studious preparations for "table talk." The notes she copied down while listening to people speak on elevated topics were to serve as a shortcut to "culture," so she could contend in conversation.

She told my client that she started keeping the red diary to keep up with Robert Kennedy's conversation when they were alone. She wanted to impress Bobby with her political grasp. She was preparing herself for a new role, she said, because Bobby had promised to make her his wife—and after he'd succeeded his brother to the presidency, "First Lady."

Marilyn's involvement with the Kennedy brothers is expressed succinctly by one sentence from the file released by the FBI: "Marilyn Monroe, the actress, first had an affair with President Kennedy, but was later passed off to his brother Robert."

During the period referred to in the file, it was not merely noted in secret government memos. In the Los Angeles summer of 1962, the affair was the not-so-discreet talk of the town. The item leaked out of the Santa Monica beach-front homes and swept down the Pacific Highway. In Brentwood, Marilyn's neighbors calmly watched the comings and goings of a tanned, skinny young man in trim slacks and open sport shirt. Once he was seen in the neighborhood in an open Cadillac convertible. The news buzzed along the Hollywood grapevine and found its way into the gossip columns. "Hollywood" was abuzz with the news.

My motive in investigating Marilyn's death was not to pass a moral judgment on Bobby, Jack, Marilyn, or anyone else connected with the case. For the purposes of my inquiry, the only thing that mattered about the liaison involving the Kennedys and Marilyn was its possible effect on her mental state and on her death. In this connection, we must look at the types of affairs that exist. Some are like calm blissful days. Some bring tonic like a refreshing shower. And some, like Marilyn's with Bobby, burst like a volcano of vengefulness, bringing disruption and chaos and death.

Dozens of books have been written about the affair and all go to great lengths to pinpoint and describe the connection. For our purposes, we need only recall that not too long ago Hollywood was a kind of "reservation" where the world's most desirable women were gathered in one place. Joseph Kennedy began the family tradition of periodic escapes from the Seaboard for the Coast with its sensuous Southern California paradise. John and Bobby's father came to Hollywood in the Twenties, invested in films, and had numerous romances with movie stars, including one with Gloria Swanson, the Marilyn Monroe of that era.

John Kennedy discovered Hollywood in the late Forties after his discharge from the Navy. He broke into the swing of the town with an actor friend, with whom he stayed. On repeat visits, he got to know the goddesses of those days, such as Gene Tierney, Rhonda Fleming and Janet Leigh. After Jack Kennedy's death, his name was openly linked to Jayne Mansfield, Kim Novak and Angie Dickinson; and for the first time a columnist felt free to use a quote in which Marilyn Monroe's relationship with the president was no longer hinted at but plainly spelled out. Some accounts place Jack Kennedy's meeting with Marilyn as early as 1951, when she was still a struggling actress with a few B-movies to her name and a fair collection of photographs, mostly as a bathing beauty. My client Robert Slatzer dates the definite beginning of Jack Kennedy's romance with Marilyn to sometime around the mid-Fifties, when Jack Kennedy was a senator, and she had just divorced DiMaggio.

The affair continued sporadically through the Fifties and lasted into Kennedy's presidency. Its high point came when Marilyn sang "Happy Birthday" at the Democrats' massive fund-raising "salute" on JFK's 45th birthday at Madison Square Garden in the spring of 1961. According to author Anthony Summers, John Kennedy had the habit of celebrating his political victories in discreet past-gala rendezvous with America's symbolic sex icon. But following the "birthday salute," their meetings grew less frequent until, because of combined FBI and family pressure, he broke the connection entirely.

It was during Marilyn's performance at Madison Square Garden that Bobby began his "dodging" around her "like a moth around the flame," as Arthur Schlesinger quoted Adlai Stevenson in his Robert Kennedy biography. Schlesinger added that Bobby "met her again at Patricia Lawford's house in Los Angeles. She called him thereafter in Los Angeles, using an assumed name. . . . One feels that Robert Kennedy came to inhabit the fantasies of her last summer. She dreamily told her friend W.J. Weatherby of the *Manchester Guardian* that she might get married again; someone in politics, in Washington . . ."

Schlesinger's guarded prose notwithstanding, Bobby, by all accounts, was instantly smitten. Through the years, friends and associates of Bobby have stopped denying it, giving the excuse that Marilyn was Robert Kennedy's "one serious extramarital romance."

To Marilyn, Robert looked like a rich college boy, he had "finish." He was nice, but "calculating," she thought. Later she was to reveal that, unlike his older brother who she complained had no time for "foreplay," being always on the run, Bobby was "boyish and cheerful in bed." These were the sorts of things she was talking about to different people a year later, and the importance of this gossip lies not in the voyeuristic detail but in the fact that she was talking freely on a subject that should have remained quiet.

Robert Kennedy was far from the only man to be fascinated and bewitched the night of the birthday salute to his brother. Marilyn had never looked more seductive, according to those present. Literally sewn into a skintight sequined gown that made her whole contour glitter, she was no longer sexual but the abstraction of sex. Marilyn, in a whispery, strangely fluty voice, to the tune of "Thanks for the Memory," wistfully sang "Thanks, Mr. President." John Kennedy sat in the Olympian balcony smoking a cigar.

"Thanks, Mr. President" was her swan song to a romance. It was the end of an affair. I believe, corroborated by everything I've been told and read, that Marilyn was truly in love with Jack. According to one version, Bobby's meeting with Marilyn occurred when Jack sent him to announce that it was over between them. At any rate, by carrying on with Robert she seized the means to remain close to John, and close to the First Family by whom, in her mind, she'd already been adopted.

John remained king, so Marilyn could not become queen. She would settle for princess with Bobby.

Marilyn's obsession with the Kennedys was like the dream of an orphan for a fairy-tale family. With regard to the Kennedys, Marilyn could not be expected to think or act rationally—they were her fantasy world.

At the time, probably no one, not even Dr. Greenson, Marilyn's psychiatrist, had greater awareness of her unreasoning state and agonized more over it than my client Robert Slatzer. I was allowed to read his first unpublished manuscript. That he led me to speculate on the different course Marilyn's life might have taken had she listened to him on that day she sought him out because she needed to talk to someone about Bobby. It was then, three weeks before her death, that she had showed him the red diary.

Bob's advice had been "to pull out of the Kennedy mess."

Bob was desperately trying to help Marilyn see reality that day in mid-July 1962. They'd driven up the Pacific Coast Highway to the beach at Point Dume. There they'd talked for hours. He was Marilyn's old and trusted friend, with the capacity to sit quietly and listen. When they met in 1946, she was still Norma

Jeane Dougherty, a shy, twenty-year-old photographic model who wanted to break into movies. Briefly Bob Slatzer from Columbus, Ohio, had enjoyed the privilege which Aphrodite grants few mortals, and for my client Marilyn's spell never wore off. She could count on his devotion, and when something troubled her, she could always call Bob. With Bob there was no need to pretend, because he would be always faithful. With him, as with few others, she could be herself.

Marilyn said she was troubled over Bobby. She'd always been able to reach him at the Department of Justice, but now she was cut off. The private number had been disconnected. She was slightly hysterical, almost in tears. Bobby had had his private number disconnected, Slatzer learned, less than twenty-four hours after Marilyn had mentioned to him that she was keeping "notes" to prep her conversation.

Bob saw how deeply hurt she was. The most painful thing in her life had always been rejection. She was 36 years old; the "shine" was fading, her looks were beginning to dull. Bitter lines had suddenly set around her mouth. Her laugh sounded coarse, and caused her lips to undergo contortions. She looked so different from the time she had greeted Bob excitedly, exulting, "Bobby Kennedy promised to marry me! What do you think of that?"

My belief that Marilyn Monroe did not kill herself formed gradually, and during the process my best ally was not my own perseverance, nor my client's story alone, nor some of the evidence that began to build up loosely to suggest the pattern of a cover-up. Of all my assistants, time proved the most useful.

Many facts connected to the Marilyn Conspiracy could not be verified immediately after her death.

Some have taken nearly a quarter century to emerge; others may never surface. It was, therefore, with great interest that I followed the proceedings of the 1975 Senate Intelligence Committee headed by Senator Frank Church. The committee was investigating alleged subversive actions by the CIA, and some details that came out of the hearings sounded familiar. Three years earlier I'd heard them described by my client, as he related to me what he had seen in the red diary under the fading sun on the beach with Marilyn at Point Dume.

Toward evening, Marilyn finished pouring out to Bob her hurt and anger. She wondered if her failure with Bobby was because she was not "educated." In her anger, she threatened to "tell all" to Bobby's wife. Bob again advised her to forget the whole thing, to get on with her life, to write it off. Then, from her handbag she pulled out a small book with a red cover. She said he might be interested to look at some of the things Bobby was discussing with her.

As my client flipped the pages, his eyes caught the entry: Bobby told me today, "I want to put that S.O.B. Jimmy Hoffa into jail, no matter how I do it." He lit on a reference to the Bay of Pigs which piqued his curiosity. He asked Marilyn what it meant. The failure of the Bay of Pigs invasion the previous year had been the Kennedy administration's first serious setback. Jack Kennedy had taken the blame for failing to provide air cover for the Cuban invaders. But from Marilyn, my client learned that on the day of the invasion the President, suffering back pain, had let Bobby run the operation, and it was Bobby who had refused to lend air cover. This, in fact, infuriated certain CIA factions.

In the diary, there were further references to Cuba,

and as if to clarify, Marilyn explained that she was "frightened and confused" because Bobby had "all those gangster connections."

The diary contained names familiar from the underworld—Sam Giancana, Johnny Roselli. There was a note on the CIA participation in the assassination of Raphael Trujillo in the Dominican Republic. One entry quoted Bobby saying the United States was not going to give sanctuary to President Diem of South Vietnam. There was another entry about Bobby's vow to cause Frank Sinatra to lose his Nevada gambling license at Cal-Neva Lodge because of his alleged associations with underworld figures.

Slatzer asked if she took notes of these conversations in front of Bobby.

Marilyn said, no, she made the notes when she was "alone."

Why did Bobby dwell on his work so much? Slatzer wondered.

Marilyn said Bobby was different from Jack, who "mesmerized" her with the discussion of paintings, sailing, literature, and the "nice things in life" that interested her much more. Bobby just boasted about whom he was going after in his fight against crime, but Marilyn, determined to educate herself however she could, took it all down.

Chapter Three

THE CONNECTIONS

It struck me as odd that Marilyn set the appointment to change her will on the day of the press conference. Was she afraid for her life?

I took on my client Bob Slatzer without a fee because in the Marilyn Conspiracy I saw the kind of case which to a detective is most appealing: it satisfies his desire to correct a wrong, while providing challenge to his professional acumen.

For over a decade, I followed the windings of the Marilyn Conspiracy. My client was an invaluable help. He and I slowly put the puzzle together. We had no book contracts, no big network, no fat newspaper behind us. This did not prevent us from doing the necessary footwork. Without great resources, it just took a bit longer. We did our stakeouts, chased down leads, and talked to mystery people whom we assumed used false names. We collected, compiled, charted, and "badgered." We badgered the L.A. Police Department, the FBI, CIA, L.A. County, and the L.A. Board of Supervisors.

Sometimes this led to tense confrontations, such as Bob had with L.A.'s Police Chief Parker, when confronting him with a request for Marilyn Monroe's confiscated telephone records. From the CIA, we received nice letters of appreciation for our work, but not much else. From the FBI, we got intriguing documents with most of the sentences "leaded out."

We discovered fresh witnesses. There were meetings with mysterious informants. Some people, like the unfathomable "Jack Quinn" and the equally mysterious "Tom," learning of our work, came forward. We had experts analyze the pathology, toxicology and Coroner's reports. I had done my own psychological "profiles" of the chief characters. We learned about the "Miner Memorandum." In the sequence of events, the outlines of a cover-up emerged.

Our first task was to narrow down our area of investigation. We concerned ourselves only with main and supporting characters. Beginning with the latter, the crucial names were those of Dr. Ralph Greenson Marilyn's psychiatrist, and Peter Lawford. Dr. Greenson died six years ago; Lawford died in 1984. Both men were important in Marilyn's last year. The psychiatrist was the first to pronounce Marilyn a "suicide," even though there had been no inquest or investigation. Peter Lawford could probably have given us the most reliable version of what happened that night; but during his life he stuck by the same improbable story, even though it changed constantly as the years went by. When he died, he took with him to the grave the secrets of Marilyn's final hours.

It's well known that in the early Sixties, when his brothers-in-law were the President and the Attorney General, Peter Lawford kept open house to the Kennedys. His Santa Monica beach house overlooking the ocean was just a few miles from Marilyn at Helena Drive. It had formerly been the home of movie mogul Louis B. Mayer. For several years before Marilyn's death, Lawford's spectacular mansion, with its view, breeziness, and cozy little rooms, provided the common ground where Jack and Bobby met Marilyn.

Lawford and Marilyn had known each other since the early Fifties, but by all accounts they were not exactly "friends." In the end, Marilyn mistrusted all men, but with Lawford the mistrust went deeper. They both came up in Hollywood at about the same time, an actor and an actress bumping into each other while looking for jobs, or at parties where the known and unknown mingled. Peter, the son of a British officer down-on-his-luck, looked handsome and, after a so-so movie career, married Pat Kennedy, Jack's and Bobby's sister.

Marilyn liked gentlemen and she didn't think Lawford, despite his appearance, was one. In his house, there were prostitutes and orgies, she complained. She complained further that Lawford provided girls for the Kennedy brothers when they came to the Coast. Frank Sinatra understood women. Yves Montand had been gentle. Jack Kennedy overwhelmed. They treated her with respect. She felt Peter Lawford "used" people. He lived in a drugged, alcoholic haze.

Perhaps in her final year, when she was a frequent guest at Lawford's mansion, Marilyn saw in her host something of herself. Mentally and physically, she'd hit a low and was falling lower. Marilyn stumbled through Lawford's rooms, men had to carry her, she passed out and lay in a stupor.

Marilyn's stardom was a burden that she could not live without. It made her simultaneously happy and unhappy. Over the years, she grew more nervous, frightened and confused. Only the heaviest sedations, the most numbing nerve depressants in astounding doses, mixed with vodka or gin, could pacify the terrors. She was both a sex symbol pulsing in light and a child in the dark who could not sleep. Her nerves, the divisions, the avalanches of mood, the two beings inside her—Norma Jeane and Marilyn—would not give her peace. She always had this fatalism, that never would she be happy. She lay in the dark and could not sleep, but she wanted to sleep because then she could dream. Barbiturates and alcohol helped her sleep, and made even wakefulness seem like sleep, and life like a dream.

My client recalled when Marilyn took her first Seconal around 1948. She was twenty-two, and nervous about her first full talking role. Bob Slatzer knew as well as anyone how much sleeping pills were a part of Hollywood in those days. He once compiled a list of stars who died of barbiturate overdose; they added up to an astonishing number.

Marilyn's barbiturate addiction from the mid-Fifties until her death was a matter of public record, splashed in headlines with each of her rescues from a comatose condition. Bob, who saw her constantly through the years, realized that the problem was becoming increasingly serious. He blamed the doctors. During her life, Marilyn had dozens of them and paid them a small fortune. Bob did not believe they did much good. He suspected that, rather than breaking her addiction, they encouraged it by prescribing more and more pills, along with giving her injections.

Bob's suspicions were unexpectedly confirmed by the red diary, which Marilyn had let him look at briefly that day on the beach at Point Dume. All the entries he saw had to do with Bobby and the politics of the day, except one that seemed to be personal. It mentioned the names of the two doctors who were treating Marilyn: her psychiatrist, Dr. Greenson, and her internist, Dr. Engelberg. In something of an aside to herself, Marilyn had noted shrewdly that while the psychiatrist claimed he was trying to get her off barbiturates, the physician kept writing prescriptions for pills which he told her she needed.

Marilyn readily saw the contradiction, but told Bob she could not bring herself to seek an explanation from either doctor, because she "trusted" them. And Bob knew all too well how desperately Marilyn needed to be able to "trust," especially those she charged with the care of her divided being. She had always required the attendance of both the doctor of the body and the doctor of the soul. In the last months of her life, their services became indispensable. And as at this point Marilyn's mind seemed to stand in the greater danger, Dr. Greenson became one of the most important men in her life.

Marilyn had been seeing Dr. Greenson, her "California" psychiatrist, since 1960. He was able to pull her through *The Misfits,* but failed to do the same for *Something's Got to Give,* Marilyn's last, uncompleted movie from which she was fired. She was brought to Dr. Greenson from the set in a comatose condition, so heavily sedated that she could hardly stand up. Before the cameras, she'd spoken her lines in a slurred, incomprehensible jumble.

I have always felt that Marilyn, for all her expressed ignorance of political affairs, was politically more knowledgeable than was generally thought. She did not read newspapers or watch television, except for an occasional special. But she knew how to evaluate political events and give them their just worth.

She had learned her politics from men. She was able to move through many worlds where politics in all its shades and complexities was always in the air. In the mid-Fifties, married and living in New York, her political education began by watching her husband, Arthur Miller, being grilled by the House Un-American Activities Committee over past Communist associations. She was a creature of Hollywood, and Hollywood in the early Fifties with its Communist witch hunts was rife with politics. She was drawn to politicians, like most movie people; politicians were "show" people, like herself. She had affairs with the president and attorney general. She was intimate with Kennedy's Hollywood friends, like Peter Lawford and Frank Sinatra. In her own politics, she was for the underdog. The Kennedy promise to make life better for the poor enthralled her, and this aspect of the Kennedy mystique which conformed to her own rudimentary political convictions was no doubt of some influence in her feeling for both brothers.

Marilyn Monroe had a very good idea of the political value of her diary entries. She was quite aware that the information she planned to make public at her press conference would ruin the Kennedys' political futures. The state secrets she had were sticks of dynamite. I don't think she was so ingenuous as to be ignorant of the dangers she was likely to bring onto herself. But something more than the fury of a woman scorned, the passion for revenge, not just on Bobby but on all men, had diminished her judgment. She was no longer completely rational. There were still streaks of lucidity within the gray, drugged mass, but the power of reasoning they lent gave way to a warped sense of jealousy that made her calculate what damage she could do to Jack and Bobby.

The evening before she died, speaking to my client, she was lucid in that strange, warped way. She told Bob Slatzer that on the following Monday, the day of the press conference, she had an appointment with "Mickey" Rudin, her lawyer, to have some changes made in her will. She wanted to make some provisions for Dr. Greenson's family because they were "nice." She wanted to bequeath some items to my client as sentimental tokens.

It struck me as odd that Marilyn set the appointment to change her will on the day of the press conference. Had she an inkling? Was she afraid for her life?

It's my feeling that she had a foreboding of her murder. In one way, she knew very well the importance of her diary entries, and she also knew the tremendous scandal she would cause with her disclosures. In the days before her death, she grew increasingly distraught and disoriented. Dr. Greenson saw her in the early evening hours before her death. She was in a "drugged" state. Her mental condition required attention, and the psychiatrist had the housekeeper stay over that night, so she could keep a close eye on the distracted patient. Marilyn felt divided and afraid. She was planning to have dinner with one of her entourage, the masseur, but Dr. Greenson did not permit it.

In the weeks before she died, Marilyn was more than distracted. Her disappointments, professionally and romantically, drove her close to a state of madness. She also had fears and a foreboding. She was rational enough to know where her fears came from. Twice, in the days before she died, she said her file cabinet was broken into. On the very day of her death, she placed a call to a local lock company for yet another change in her lock combination. She'd already discussed the idea of the press conference with a "close friend." She told my client, "Bobby owes me an explanation for walking out on me like that."

I wondered if Bobby knew of the method by which she was going to demand an answer, and who else knew of her disordered mental condition. Who else had been informed of the press conference? The man Marilyn knew most intimately, Frank Sinatra, and her friends the Lawfords were also friends of the Kennedys. And there were yet further channels through which information could reach the other names mentioned in her diary: Sam "Momo" Giancana, Mafia "boss of bosses," successor to Al Capone, and his West Coast lieutenant, Johnny Roselli.

Marilyn Monroe knew too much. As my client expressed it, "She was in over her head." Her mental state during her final weeks was well-known to many people. She was irrational, and she knew too much. That made her "unreliable." And led to her death.

Marilyn's state of mind during this time was of chief concern to Dr. Greenson. He had been treating her for over two years, and in the end their relationship grew beyond the doctor-patient stage to a family friendship.

After her death, Dr. Greenson implied that if his patient had not been Marilyn Monroe she would have been committed to a "lunatic asylum." He stated that when Marilyn first came to him she was using the nerve depressant sodium pentothal, the morphine-like Demerol, barbiturate phenobarbital and Nembutal sleeping pills. His diagnosis: "psychotic manifestations," "schizophrenia," "depressive" and "paranoid" reactions.

Dr. Greenson's testimony to Marilyn's condition was given out after Marilyn died and was quickly accepted as medical sanction of the cause of death. Until he passed away in 1979, Dr. Greenson maintained that Marilyn committed suicide because of her inability to handle "rejection." Because Marilyn's fear of "rejection," barbiturate addiction, and sleeping nude had been well-publicized and were generally known, it sounded plausible. Yet my investigation revealed numerous inconsistencies that in Marilyn's case make "plausibility" a substitute for the truth.

The fact that Marilyn was mentally unstable in the end was given as the standard explanation by Dr. Greenson, L.A. County Coroner Dr. Theodore Curphey and L.A. Police Department Chief William Parker. For twenty years, it stood as the official word. I agree that Marilyn gave strong evidence of being mentally unstable at the time of her death, but not all mentally unstable people kill themselves. Marilyn was known to be addicted to barbiturates, but on the night of August 4, the evidence proves she did not "overdose" herself.

All the facts of Marilyn's life which were known to the public—her history of near-suicides and pill-taking, even the fact that she slept nude—made "suicide" look plausible. Our own study of the Coroner's and police reports, however, led us to conclude otherwise, and our suspicions were confirmed by various witnesses, such as the deputy coroner's aide Lionel Grandison. After signing the death certificate, he mysteriously vanished until discovered by my client. The even more mysterious Jack Quinn saw the official police report and told my client, "Bobby lied like a bastard, and not only that, so did the actor." The Miner Memorandum, a document of extreme significance, shows the cover-up might have started in the D.A.'s office. The president of the ambulance service gave us direct evidence that supported our conclusion from the study of the Coroner's report that Marilyn Monroe had died as the result of a fatal injection.

Early in the investigation I heard that an ambulance service was involved in Marilyn's death. This rumor in one instance led the kind of young man I call a "clown" to attempt to convince me that he had been the ambulance driver. He was subjected to a polygraph test. The needle almost jumped off the gauge, and he was shown to the door. He then went to a widely circulated tabloid, and sold the story for $40,000. When in protest I called the editor, he said, "It sells papers." Eventually, I located Walter Schaefer, president of the ambulance service which dispatched a vehicle to Marilyn's house on the night she died. With each false lead, in this case the fake ambulance driver, there's an effect of a ripple spreading, and eventually "someone who knows someone," a person who wishes to remain anonymous will come along with a confession.

While a consultant on ABC's 20/20, I managed to track down an ambulance driver in Los Angeles by the name of Murray Liebowitz. He was asked if he'd taken Marilyn's body to a hospital and then returned it to her home. He became instantly incommunicado, saying he wished to have nothing to do with anything concerning Marilyn. He refused to go on camera; afterward, I heard he changed his name to Lieb, not that it mattered, for the show was never aired. I think it was a documentary that would have made a mark in television. I've never seen anything comparable in shock value. I believe it would not just change our way of looking at a notorious, real-life Hollywood drama, but our whole thinking about the Camelot years.

Some time afterward, we heard from Ken Hunter, who said he had been Liebowitz's partner. He said that he and Liebowitz worked for the same company and that they were on duty the night of August 4. In the early morning hours, they picked up Marilyn Monroe "in a comatose state," at her home in Brentwood. From Hunter I went to Walter Schaefer in October 1985. Schaefer was the president of the ambulance service I'd spent years tracking down.

"You know for certain," I asked, "that your ambulance picked up Marilyn Monroe on the night of her death?"

"Absolutely sure," Schaefer said.

"How can you be?"

"We had records."

Walter Schaefer confirmed that Liebowitz and Hunter picked up Marilyn Monroe, but that the transport records were destroyed as part of routine operations some years later. I asked him where his people took Marilyn, and at what time. She was taken to Santa Monica Hospital around 2:00 A.M., he recalled, though he was not positive of the exact time.

"Are you certain?" I asked, astonished.

Calmly, Schaefer said, "There's no question."

"What did your crew do with her?"

"Took her to the ER (Emergency Room), then left."

Schaefer said Marilyn was "comatose but still alive." This was not the first time, he added, that his company had picked up Marilyn in this condition. He believed she was not "naked," though not having been there, he couldn't be sure.

"Where did she die?" I asked.

"At the hospital, of course."

"The Santa Monica Hospital?" I repeated, still incredulous. Schaefer said yes.

I asked, "Did you return her dead body to her home?"

He shook his head.

My client had spoken to Schaefer earlier, and after learning this mind-boggling news, asked why he had not told his story before. In his answer, Schaefer gave the impression that what really happened in Hollywood, at least back in 1962, often never got reported.

After I demanded an investigation into Marilyn Monroe's death on August 4, 1982, the L.A. Board of Supervisors ordered the District Attorney to look into the case. About seven weeks later, I had a "secret" meeting with Deputy District Attorney Ronald M. "Mike" Carroll, who would soon be dismissing some of the most convincing witnesses and, after a review, deciding that the case did not merit reopening by the Grand Jury. I had not told Carroll of my own investigation, but when I came into his office, I found him surprisingly up to date. The first thing he said was, "What do you know about this ambulance driver claiming to have picked up Monroe?"

He looked at me in an apprehensive manner, and that would remain his attitude throughout the "review."

In the world of the detective, verification of fact is most difficult to come by. The majority of my clients are attorneys. The facts I collect for them demand the highest standard of truthfulness to be admissible as evidence in courts. Bob and I gathered our facts on Marilyn's death over the years according to these standards. In 1974 we called for the Grand Jury to reopen the Marilyn case. It was not until almost another ten years had gone by, on the twentieth anniversary of Marilyn's mysterious demise, that we felt our evidence was strong enough to demand again a formal inquest into her death by the Grand Jury.

When Bob Slatzer and I introduced our preliminary findings on the critical disappearance of the red diary to the public, it started a series of sensational events in Los Angeles. This furor led the L.A. County Board of Supervisors to order the District Attorney to open an investigation into Marilyn's death. The worldwide attention that was focused on my investigation sparked the best-selling book *Goddess* by British journalist Anthony Summers, who said that it was my investigation of the cover-up that inspired his work, and gave renewed interest to the events surrounding Marilyn's death.

Summers' book, which uses many of my results on the investigation of the cover-up, brought to the public's attention facts which I released in 1982, when at the L.A. Press Club I first raised my voice to demand a reexamination of the Monroe affair. Since then, I've come up with additional facts which should persuade the Grand Jury or the District Attorney to open the investigation into Marilyn's death. I have evidence that the possibility of murder cannot be ruled out.

Together, Bob and I spent thirteen years to come to this conclusion. It took so long, not because the story did not become clear until the end of the investigation—the story was known at a very early stage—but because a story without "evidence" is hearsay and rumor. Many rumors had sprung up around Marilyn's grave; like a chorus, they breathed the same names.

Of the greatest interest to us were the "rumors" that came from inside the L.A. Police Department and the

District Attorney's office. Within these two great bureaucratic camps, the rumors over the handling of the case had become legend. The "legend" corroborated a Kennedy/CIA/Mafia entanglement around Marilyn, which soon became the most persistent motif in my investigation.

I kept hearing about it from what I consider extremely reliable sources, colleagues paying respect to one of the brotherhood. For example, one detective who'd handled the paperwork on Marilyn's death would convey to me confidentially that the police reports on the investigation of the case were filled with Kennedy's name. From yet another "contact" at the D.A.'s office I would hear about what at the time was dismissed as the ravings of the lunatic fringe—that back in 1962 the Mafia and the CIA collaborated in covering up what really happened during the night of Marilyn's death.

Though all these "rumors" turned out to be extremely valuable, I could not accept them at the time as "admissible evidence." In order to "stand up" they required proof from the most unimpeachable sources. Such proof, I realized, could originate only from official quarters. Until this was forthcoming, our investigation necessarily came to a halt.

Perseverance and patience helped us amass information on the local level. Within the L.A. bureaucracy we had our "contacts." But when it came to demonstrating a possible CIA/Mafia connection in Marilyn's death, we felt inadequate to the magnitude of the task. But here again, time came to the rescue. We were three years into our investigation before we got our big "break." As I had expected, it came from official quarters, and it encouraged us to continue our probe, since it confirmed one of Marilyn's diary entries and her concerns expressed to my client about Bobby's "gangster connections."

Our big "break" did not so much confirm facts as establish "motive," which is the first question a detective must ask. The evidence we sought came from the 1975 Senate Intelligence Committee investigation of the CIA. The committee found that in the early Sixties there had been a link between the Mafia and the Office of the Attorney General, and that certain members of the underworld were on the government payroll.

A few years later, under a different administration, Jimmy Hoffa was convicted of running a gangster-controlled labor union. This was our second break in connective with "motive."

In the end, we were able to see the "big picture." It showed that the Kennedys, the CIA and the Mafia were collaborating on some levels and opposing each other on others. This picture conformed to what Bob had seen in the little red diary and what Marilyn had told him. It led us to believe that there were people in the highest precincts of power, both legal and criminal, who might share a joint interest in silencing a threat that in different ways concerned them all, the hurtful accusations of an aging sex symbol who distrusted men and believed that Bobby "owed her an explanation."

Chapter Four

THE BODY

"I just had another abortion . . . I don't know if it was Bobby's or Jack's."

In the early hours of August 5, 1962, someone called the Hocketts at Westwood Memorial Cemetery. The caller identified himself as Lionel Grandison, deputy coroner's aide to L.A. County Coroner, Dr. Theodore Curphey. It was Grandison's job to take "first calls" on deaths occurring in L.A. County, particularly those that looked suspicious. This was routine for L.A. County when a person died without a physician's direct attendance. In that case, a medical examiner from the Coroner's Office checked the circumstances of death.

Grandison reported to his supervisor, and the body of Marilyn Monroe was determined to require follow-up investigation by the County Coroner and the L.A. City Police Department. In the early morning, it was rushed from Westwood to the L.A. Coroner's office downtown at the Hall of Justice on Temple Street. There the world's most famous body received a number—Coroner's Case No. 81128—and it was moved to Crypt 33 at the County Morgue.

At 10:30 A.M. on August 5, 1962, the knife of the Deputy Coroner Examiner, Dr. Thomas Noguchi, severed Marilyn's facial muscles in order to remove the brain. With scalpel and saw he removed specimens of organs to be tested by the toxicologist. He took samples of blood and liver materials for Dr. Abernathy, the chief toxicologist. Four days later, Dr. Noguchi, signing his autopsy report, circled under the column marked Mode of Death, "Suicide." But then, perhaps thinking better of it, he penciled in the word "probable."

Marilyn's body could now be laid to rest. Her death had been attested to by an obscure name, Lionel Grandison, whose bearer was shortly to vanish. Dr. Curphey, the County Coroner, who had taken personal charge of Marilyn's case, appointed a Suicide Investigation Team to study Marilyn's death; it did not occur to him that, with the same degree of probability, he might have called it a Murder Investigation Team. But the D.A., the Police and the Coroner's Office were in agreement that Marilyn had died by her own hand. The County was satisfied that the requirements had been met. On paper at least, Marilyn's death was in order. Everything official, without which a body cannot enter upon eternity, had been done.

Yet Marilyn's body refused to depart. Her body was public and her life was a parable, an American parable of money, power, sex and death.

The Hollywood Marilyn knew at midcentury was still built around a legend that everyone believed in. It was about a pretty girl who dreams of becoming a movie star and one day, in some ordinary place like a drugstore or parking lot, she's "discovered." It actually did happen that way frequently enough, and it is typical of Marilyn that she conformed to the legend, for the legend became her life.

Her star set over the declining days of the Old Hollywood, when the studios still ruled hordes of starlets known as "contract players." At her death, Marilyn was still under "contract" to Twentieth Century Fox, and anxious to complete the film that would release her. She died without finishing her "contract." Marilyn Monroe was Old Hollywood's last total creation, and when she died the Old Hollywood died with her.

Bob Slatzer came to the film capital to escape having to go into his father's paint-contracting business. At fourteen, he had already decided that he wanted to be a reporter in Hollywood. John Barrymore is to be held largely responsible for this as, passing through Bob's hometown in Ohio, the famous actor granted Bob an interview for his junior high school newspaper. Six years later, Bob arrived in Hollywood and soon met a girl who was likewise a worshiper of Barrymore. Both were then living on Hollywood's hungry fringes. Bob chased movie gossip for his Ohio newspaper, and Marilyn chased important men in the studios who could give her jobs. Bob lent the pretty starlet a biography on Barrymore which she devoured. She said Barrymore was the "perfect actor." Bob and Norma Jeane were barely twenty; they were starstruck and on their dates they went out to gaze at the houses of their movie heroes.

Marilyn wanted to be an actress. In 1944, she was "discovered" while working on the assembly line at a defense plant in the San Fernando Valley. She told

Bob the story, which is so much like the beginning of a fairy tale: a photographer spots a pretty girl in overalls; she's a voluptuous eighteen-year-old with a pile of blond curls, radiating health and looking like a fruit ready to be plucked; her photos begin appearing as "morale boosters" in Armed Forces magazines; the voluptuous girl goes on to "pinups" and "cheesecake" wearing bottoms and tops and shorts and tight sweaters; and always beneath the blond curls there's that smile that seems to be coyly provoking. With this innocent image, Norma Jeane became a popular pinup in the tame girlie magazines of those days. The voluptuous girl was still a child. She did not threaten. She had something vulnerable, open, soft. Her sexuality was not sultry and complex. It was like an advertisement for something refreshing and sweet that bubbled.

It would be only partly true, however, to say that Marilyn was "discovered." Marilyn discovered herself by discovering the perfection of her own body. At sixteen, she noticed its effect on her young husband, the first to be seized by the passion to photograph her nude. Then she noticed that by wearing certain clinging, skimpy things and walking a certain wiggly way and thrusting out her chest, she gained everybody's attention. After this discovery, she lost interest in marriage. She must have sensed that the Perfect Body is destined to conquer.

Before she became a creature of the studios, Marilyn was already her own creation. She disciplined her body into making every gesture seductive. She created herself as a sex symbol by making her whole being sexual. That was the "electricity" men felt from her. Her sexuality was "instant," like turning on a light.

* * *

THE MARILYN CONSPIRACY

During her reign as Hollywood's "Golden Girl," Marilyn Monroe was the most famous blond in the world, the sex goddess who received nearly 20,000 fan letters a week. These letters helped make her one of the most valuable "properties" in Hollywood. For in the era of the "star system" some thirty years ago, when Hollywood was far more glamorous and colorful than today, a star's popularity actually was measured by the amount of fan mail generated.

A team of high-powered publicists at the studio manufactured the Marilyn Monroe image and sold it round the world. It was their job to keep her photos and stories in print during the promotion of her films, as well as in between pictures. Marilyn Monroe became a "commodity." Her "myth" was part and parcel of the "star system." The moviegoing audiences, enthralled by the myth, flocked to Marilyn's pictures, and she became celebrated as the undisputed sex goddess of all time. Marilyn Monroe even surpassed Jean Harlow, and all the others who had preceded her, as the unchallenged mistress of the silver screen.

Marilyn's early image differed from that of her later career. The fan magazines and news stories portrayed her as the beautiful girl who lived in a small apartment and cooked her own meals. While dreaming of the ideal man, she spent weekend nights sitting at home, waiting for the phone to ring, hoping it would be someone asking her for a date. Perhaps it might be the man of her dreams, the man she would eventually marry, who would take her away from the plastic of Tinsel Town so she could have the family she had always wanted. . . .

About ten years later, Lena Pepitone, Marilyn's devoted maid in New York, heard the real story from

the star's own mouth, as she reminisced about breaking into the studios when she couldn't act and all she
had was "blond hair and a body men liked." Singers,
actresses, prostitutes—Marilyn said it was the same.
"They all get started the same way. At least I did."
There were the customary inspections by the influential studio people of all the new starlets. "The worst
thing a girl could do," Marilyn told Lena, "was to say
no to one of these guys."

Her first contract was with Twentieth Century Fox,
whose founder Joe Schenck was known for buying any
woman he desired. Marilyn got her start through
Schenck, then bald and over 70 years old, who had her
come over to his mansion on so many visits that in the
Hollywood press their names became "romantically"
linked. Marilyn recalled he "seemed to have this thing
about breasts." After dinner, he told her Hollywood
stories, and she sat spellbound listening to wonderful
tales about John Barrymore, Charlie Chaplin, Valen-
tino, all the stars, while Mr. Schenck played with her
breasts. "He didn't want to do much else," Marilyn
confided to her maid, "since he was getting old, but
sometimes he asked me to kiss him—down there. . . .
It would seem like hours, and nothing would happen,
but I was afraid to stop. I felt like gagging, but I
thought if I did he'd get insulted." All her rival starlets
were envious, and Marilyn kept visiting Schenck,
because in those hungry days, at least "the food was
good."

Schenck gave Marilyn her first billing in *Dangerous
Years*. He next introduced her to Harry Cohn, boss of
Columbia Pictures, for whom she did *Ladies of the
Chorus*, a film in which she had her first full-length
talking role as well as the chance to dance and sing. In
the film she made for Cohn, she sang "Every baby

needs a Da-Da." "Mr. Cohn," Marilyn told Lena, "wasn't the kind who even said hello first. He just told you to get in bed."

After making several more pictures, Marilyn got her big chance in *The Asphalt Jungle*, the 1950 John Huston film that brought her first big public acclaim. For her next film, Schenck introduced her to Darryl Zanuck, and she became an "overnight sensation" in his *All About Eve*. Marilyn Monroe made fourteen more films before she played in a production called *Niagara* in 1952, which coincided with the publication of the then notorious "nude calendar."

Until *Niagara*, Marilyn Monroe had played mostly bit parts, leaving on each a stronger stamp of the blond sexual image. As some Hollywood hands had shrewdly foreseen, the "nude calendar" made her a star. In *Niagara*, she did her customary undulating in tight skirts, but after the calendar and the sensational publicity, she was at once promoted to top billing.

The calendar is still selling today. In its best-known pose, "Golden Dream," Marilyn Monroe lies stretched lengthwise on a burnished velvet spread, in a maelstrom of suggestively rippling cloth. Her pale body lies with the blond head thrown back, the lips parted, open and vulnerable, as if inviting ravishment. The "nude calender" brought stardom, establishing Marilyn Monroe as the sex symbol whose sexuality did not threaten. In her greatest movies, such as *Gentlemen Prefer Blondes*, *How to Marry a Millionaire*, *There's No Business Like Show Business*, *The Seven Year Itch*, *Bus Stop*, and *Some Like It Hot*, the plots are simple, sometimes poignant and usually funny, but what makes them memorable is the presence of a coy creature, the orphan with the Perfect Body.

With the body and blond freshness, Norma Jeane

wiggled her way onto the movie set. She paid the price of admission with the only possession she had, trading herself to studio bosses, agents and producers, photographers, publicists, reporters, to all men, young and old, who could help get her jobs or get her photos into the news. The studios took her dreary history and packaged it into a ready-made item. To all who wished to hear it, she told the story of the orphan, the vanished father, the foster homes, because that was the story the studios liked. After she became famous, she fought the Hollywood bosses to get better terms and greater choice of movie roles. But in the early years, she obeyed because the studios were all-powerful, and so in every interview she ran dutifully through the recital of her bleak times.

The movies made Marilyn famous, but like everything else in her life, when she achieved her goal, she found it lacking. She set out to reap fame, but when it came to her as an acclaimed "comedienne," she discovered that it was not the kind of fame she wanted. "Comedienne" meant "dumb blonde," and she felt humiliated. She alone knew the secrets of her success. She knew what it had cost her, and how she'd been humiliated. In the end, she hated Hollywood for having taken everything from her—her name and her past and her body.

After her death, Darryl Zanuck, her old boss at Twentieth Century Fox, said, "Nobody discovered her; she earned her own way to stardom."

What he meant is understood only in Hollywood. He meant that Marilyn paid for everything.

Her body was perfect and every man wanted it.

Today, the Hollywood star is a "personality" and his life is mostly his own concern. But until some twenty-five years ago, the stars' lives were public. Their lives off-screen often were more dramatic than their movies. In the Fifties, Marilyn's tragedies were turned into media events staged by studios. Her nervous collapses and near-suicides, her affairs, marriages and divorces were enacted before the nation and aroused public emotion.

What Marilyn sought from men was power. There were only a few men from whom she asked simple friendship. In her world, men held power, and men were predators. But she had "stunning proportions." With her sexuality, she conquered. Men became her slaves and she became the slave of men, because she always needed men in order to conquer.

Marilyn's marriages were "conquests" that extended her power. They allowed her to conquer new worlds. Bob Slatzer's power was of a different sort. He and Marilyn lived two days "as man and wife." Afterward they tore up the certificate, and went back to Mexico to have the marriage annulled. "This will be our secret . . . always," Marilyn had said. About two years later, she married Joe DiMaggio, the premier baseball player of the postwar era.

With DiMaggio, Marilyn married a popular institution, an authentic hero who symbolized American patriotism. A whole nation adored the "Yankee Clipper," "Joltin' Joe," and marrying this symbol did far more for her career than the nude calendar or her films. DiMaggio got the country to accept and love Marilyn Monroe. She entered the popular imagination.

When Marilyn married DiMaggio, she became a heroine, but at home her hero behaved like a man. He liked to watch sports on television and to read the sports pages. He liked to take his stunning wife to restaurants and to have her accompany him while fishing. On certain nights, he played cards with "buddies." For relaxation, he took her to Nevada, to Las Vegas or Tahoe. He was everywhere and always jealous, and he disliked her being immodest on film.

The marriage broke up not because Joe was jealous, but because Marilyn was restless. The hero was too dull for Marilyn's tastes, and after nine months their marriage ended with Marilyn weeping at a press conference while making the announcement. Until her death, however, DiMaggio remained in Marilyn's life as the kind of man she occasionally needed but never wanted for long. A lot of showgirls married safe tycoons, but Marilyn could never settle for safety alone. She was a sexual adventuress, an explorer of sexual powers. She possessed a body which opened all the doors that had been closed to Norma Jeane. Marilyn was to fulfill all the fantasies dreamed of by the little girl. All her fantasies were constructed to keep out the fear and loneliness of that little girl, and each man brought her a fantasy.

Two years after divorcing DiMaggio, she married Arthur Miller, America's foremost playwright. The world he represented, of New York, art, literature and serious drama, might still the fear and loneliness and fill the emptiness. To be married to a sedate bookish man, of accomplished intellect and culture, to join her sexual being to his capacious mind, to produce children, to become a tragic actress rather than a "dumb blonde," and to live on the scintillating surface of mental ferment, was the fantasy she married. Like all her fantasies, it soon dissolved.

With her depressions and pills, her moods and temper and inexplicable bursts of mad vivacity, she bewildered the bookish man and at last became his trial. He kept to his room and produced very little. Through the four years of their marriage, she continued making films. The tall, pipe-smoking man of letters accompanied his dazzling wife on location. They lived in New York and Connecticut. In her films, Marilyn Monroe grew more gorgeous and more successful. She was studying "method acting" under the famous Lee Strasberg. But she was also collapsing and being rushed to hospitals. She never got over her anxieties. In every world, she felt rejected. There were overdoses and afterward, for a while, more judicious mixtures of alcohol and pills. "Culture," like Hollywood, like sports, was not what she had imagined, and she felt more empty and confused.

Her husband, America's great playwright, wrote a movie script for her called *The Misfits*. It was directed by John Huston and starred Clark Gable. America's foremost actor, director, and playwright joined to acknowledge her as a dramatic artist. But she was still unhappy and distraught.

Marilyn's complexes were demons that drove her to seek what she most wished to avoid. Her fear of rejection made her reach for the unattainable. She'd married men who were among America's most prominent, and their worlds had not lived up to the fantasy. After her divorce from Miller, Marilyn Monroe entered upon the tragic final year when she constructed a fantasy out of marrying a powerful politician and becoming one of the presidential family. It was the only fantasy left, and it was unattainable.

Marilyn Monroe died at thirty-six. Ten years earlier she created a sensation with her "nude calendar." The photos were printed in the first edition of a new magazine called *Playboy*, which launched the "sexual revolution" by making nudity a respectable commodity. Through those pictures, a whole nation feasted on the vision of the Perfect Body, and Marilyn Monroe became the goddess of sex. But just before she died, she seemed to be desperately seeking reassurances that the power of the goddess was not lost.

In August 1962, all of her thoughts revolved around the fantasy with Bobby. For a while, it was beautiful. Bobby came out to the Coast a lot and stayed with the Lawfords. Then she could no longer reach him. She told my client that the switchboard at the Justice Department refused to put her through. She told Bob of having heard from someone that Bobby had called her "dumb blonde or dumb broad." She needed to be reassured that her body was still perfect. In the summer of 1962, there was a sudden flurry of nude sessions with photographers for leading magazines.

When Bob Slatzer met Marilyn in 1946, she was already separated from her first husband and about to shed the name Dougherty. Norma Jeane was to become "Marilyn" after another movie star, and "Monroe" after her maternal grandfather. The studio had suggested the name change, and it was something the new Marilyn had a difficult time getting used to. By shedding our name we shed our identity, and from my professional experience, when sifting through the aliases of miscreants, I am always aware that I'm dealing with people who live under stress. This has enabled me to understand how "Marilyn" became the sex symbol's enduring identity problem, for "Marilyn" was not real, her sex image was not real, and her body was not real. It was an extraordinary dwelling from which she lived apart. Her obsession with cameras and mirrors went beyond the conventional "narcissism" attributed to her by friends, familiars and psychiatrists. It came from a constant need to know that the dwelling still stood. Marilyn was terribly afraid and insecure. She needed to be constantly reminded that she was irresistible, and at no time more so than in the final months of her life when, as if taking a last distracted look at her body, she became obsessed once more with her nudity.

Bob Slatzer said that nudity made Marilyn feel "secure." He observed that even as an unknown starlet, Marilyn, needing the constant reassurance of her body, wherever possible discarded her clothes. Early in her career, she was in the habit of giving nude interviews. Later, she became notorious for announcing that she never wore panties and slept nude. She would sometimes go out wearing a coat and nothing beneath. At home, much to the surprise of her maids and visitors, she wore no clothes. When her dead body was found, it was nude, though I believe she was placed in that condition by someone familiar with her habits.

Bob Slatzer managed to talk with the person who had arranged the nude shots, Marilyn's press aide Pat Newcomb, who at the time was an employee of Arthur Jacobs Company, one of Hollywood's top-flight public relations firms. It was one of the rare interviews given by this reticent and elusive woman, who had been one of the last to see Marilyn alive on August 4, 1962.

When we began our investigation, one of our first missions was to establish contact with those people who throughout the years had been "RTS," Reluctant to Speak. Among these were the people in Marilyn's house on the day she died. After more than a decade, the housekeeper, Mrs. Murray, was to retract her previous account of that day. But Pat Newcomb, who had frequently stayed with Marilyn and had also been present, has always stuck by the story, which was the official one, that Bobby at the time was not in Los Angeles.

Some time later we discovered that Pat Newcomb had been a friend of the Kennedy family before she met Marilyn, and that she was especially close to Bobby. It is impossible not to think of her as a likely source of privileged information, particularly after the subsequent course of her career. After Marilyn's funeral, she was flown to the Kennedy compound at Hyannisport, where she remained a guest for several weeks. I discovered that from here she vanished from sight during a six-month European tour. Upon her return, she got a job as a specialist in motion pictures for the United States Information Agency, with an office next to that of the Attorney General's. When this appeared in the newspapers, she was transferred. She later joined Robert Kennedy's staff after he resigned as Attorney General to run for the office of senator from New York State.

In the early Sixties, Pat Newcomb was usually invited by the Lawfords when the Kennedys were in town, and either Jack or Bobby would meet with Marilyn. Pat Newcomb, as press aide and "handler," arranged and directed Marilyn's final years. It was her job to watch over the sex siren like a combination mother hen and hawk. While living at Marilyn's home, she got paid by her employer, the Arthur Jacobs Company, who put her in charge of Marilyn's personal life after the agency's famous, profitable but emotionally volatile client entered upon the series of destructive fixations on unattainable men.

Bob's interview with Marilyn's close confidante proved disappointing. She remained RTS, refusing to link Bobby and Marilyn on the day of her death, despite the contrary evidence that was already mounting. However, some two decades later I was able to talk to a former colleague of hers, Michael Selsman, who had also worked at the Arthur Jacobs Company at the time. Selsman had made the funeral arrangements for the studio. Now a producer and agent, Selsman told me that Marilyn had had an abortion just a few months prior to her death. "I just had another abortion," she was quoted as saying, "I don't know if it was Bobby's or Jack's."

Selsman worked closely with Pat Newcomb, and he said it was common knowledge at the agency that Marilyn was involved with both Jack and Bobby Kennedy. It was generally believed that Bobby was the father. The agency's brass was apparently worried about what such a disclosure would do to her image.

I was directed to a prominent local hospital, where I discovered that Marilyn had been hospitalized during the period mentioned by Selsman. He'd warned me before I set out that the hospital records would list another medical reason, but I didn't need to be cautioned. Having already devoted over a decade to the Marilyn Conspiracy, I expected very little from the public records. At the hospital I discovered that, indeed, the medical reason given was not abortion. I was not surprised. I'd learned early in my investigation to ignore anything "official" concerning the death of Marilyn Monroe.

Chapter Five

THE POLITICS

There was another voice on the tape, someone calling from San Francisco . . . the voice asked, "Is she dead yet?"

Informants usually do not come forward. Normally, detectives have to go out and look for them. But in the Marilyn case we had the good fortune to attract a great number of usually anonymous but reliable witnesses. They came from all walks of life. They reached us directly or through second or third parties, and sometimes in an odd combination of people and circumstances, such as the roofer and the Marilyn Monroe look-alike.

The roofer, working at the home of an actress-night club entertainer who had once won a Marilyn Monroe look-alike contest, complimented the woman on her remarkable resemblance to the famous movie star. He told her that he'd recently fixed a leak in the Brentwood home that had been the residence of Marilyn Monroe, and casually mentioned having found in the roof a large amount of wiring and objects that looked like miniature transmitters.

THE MARILYN CONSPIRACY

The woman phoned Bob Slatzer, who got in touch with the roofer. The man confirmed that his foot had gone through a certain area on the tiled roof of Marilyn's former home. The spot had been rotted away by rain and moisture through the years, and beneath it in a shallow crawl space he'd found wiring, as well as some old rusty transmitters. The roofer said he was familiar with electronic eavesdropping equipment through training in military intelligence. He estimated that the equipment had been under the tiles between fifteen and twenty years. He said he had pulled all the wiring out and had collected the other equipment and filled a small trash can halfway.

Although we never saw the wires and electronic devices that had been thrown out, the roofer's tale checked with what we had learned from other sources during our investigation. And so we obtained yet another confirmation of the issue which by then we had established as lying at the heart of the Marilyn Conspiracy—just such a bunch of wires and bugging devices as the roofer had found in Marilyn's home fifteen years after her death.

By 1977, when I visited Marilyn Monroe's former home to check out the roofer's story, both Bob Slatzer and I had long been convinced that Marilyn Monroe in the last weeks of her life had not been deluded in supposing that her phones were tapped. What she did not know was the extent of the bugging operation. She was correct in assuming that someone was listening to her calls, but she did not know that her rooms, including her bedroom, were wired. She became paranoid and would only call from pay phones. Bob Slatzer finally begged her to leave her bag of coins at home and let him accept the charges.

Several years after Marilyn's death, he first heard of Bernard "Bernie" Bates Spindel. Known among pros as "king of the wiretappers," Spindel admitted to a source close to Slatzer having put the tap on Marilyn's home.

Spindel's role actually became public knowledge as early as December 21, 1966, in a *New York Times* article headed, "Suit Asks Return of Bugging Items, Tapes on Marilyn Monroe and Others Are Listed." It appeared that the New York State Police earlier had raided Spindel's home, and that in response in "an affidavit submitted to the court," the news item read, "Bernard Spindel asserted that some of the seized material contained tapes and evidence concerning the circumstances surrounding the death of Marilyn Monroe, which strongly suggests that the officially reported circumstances of her demise were erroneous."

When I met my informant "Tom" in the late summer of 1982, he urged, "Forget about the red diary, Milo, get the tapes." He said if the tapes were found, I'd learn that Marilyn was definitely not alone during the final minutes of her life. "Tom" gave me to understand that she was entertaining two very close and trusted friends. The two had been in her home many times before. They were there when she died. There was a phrase on the tape, "What are we going to do with her dead body?" There was another voice on the tape, someone calling from San Francisco—we knew it was San Francisco because in 1962 there was no direct dialing and the operator identified the city—the voice asked, "Is she dead yet?"

Who had the tapes?

"Tom" asked if I was familiar with the name Spindel.

"Bernie," I reminded him, hardly needing to have

my memory refreshed as to the most notorious or most famous, depending on one's point of view, of the clandestine wiretappers. In 1968, I'd read Spindel's book, *The Ominous Ear*, in which Spindel seemed to defend the citizen's right to wiretap. I wouldn't go quite so far. On the contrary. I wrote my first book, *Shhh!* on the subject of privacy invasion and how to prevent it.

The fact that I chose the subject of electronic eavesdropping as one of my first writing ventures shows how much the work of today's detective has changed in the postwar years. The modern detective is no longer the "gumshoe" of old. Electronic surveillance and wiretapping is the name of the game. For nearly a quarter century I have schooled myself in the art of countermeasures to illegal snooping devices. In 1975, I testified before the Presidential and Congressional Wiretap Commission, which helped bring about new federal laws on the subject. I felt myself qualified to judge Spindel on professional grounds, and there he was "tops." The Spindel people were absolute pros. Back in the early Sixties, Spindel was about ten years ahead of his time; the "bugs," for instance, that Spindel placed in Marilyn's bedroom, were smaller than books of matches.

Like most of the professional wiretappers, Spindel learned clandestine electronic surveillance in the military. After early training with the United States Signal Corps, he was assigned as an intelligence officer until the end of World War II. Official CIA records show Spindel was turned down when he sought employment with the agency. He then opened his own detective bureau, The B.R. Fox Company, which served as a front for his electronic surveillance activities.

The "king of the wiretappers" lived with his wife

and six children in a quiet part of New York State. He allowed his closest friends to call him "Bernie." But not even these could say they knew the "king." Spindel was essentially a loner. No one, possibly not even his wife, knew to whom he was really pledged. Everybody knew he worked for Jimmy Hoffa, and that he was a "Mafia wireman." Some actually believed that he was with the "Company." After his death, his widow learned that he was eligible for a military funeral, and she still believes he was some sort of government agent. I recalled this possible connection when told that somehow Spindel became the first American to make Dominican dictator Trujillo's "execution list." Marilyn's red diary had shown an entry concerning Trujillo and his assassination by the CIA.

In the shadowy world of wiretappers, Spindel was known for being more shadowy than most. He died in 1971 at age 45 of a heart attack, after serving a prison term for illegal wiretapping. His legend sprang from feats which earned the admiration of electronic eavesdroppers, including his adversaries. Ingenuity and cool derring-do were among his trademarks. Spindel was known to have bugged even FBI cars and police departments. He had a running battle with the Bell Telephone System, and another with the Internal Revenue Service. But he was best known for being Jimmy Hoffa's "prober," with a special assignment to "bug" Robert Kennedy.

Bob Slatzer, detecting early on the Hoffa connection, knew about Spindel and the tap on Marilyn's home. Since then a number of sources have confirmed that Spindel wired Marilyn's house for Jimmy Hoffa, who wanted to get embarrassing information on Marilyn and Robert Kennedy. This was the Teamsters' boss's obvious reply to Marilyn's diary entry, "I want to put that S.O.B. Hoffa into jail, no matter how I do it."

I thought of the "king of the wiretappers" during my investigation of the roofer's story. At Marilyn's former residence, I discovered a set of five multicolored wires in the spouting that provided the runoff for water from the roof. There was a gauge with the multicolored wires that was slightly larger than that which the telephone company might use. Ordinarily, eavesdroppers use two wires, but twenty years ago a lot of unconventional things were done. Perhaps only two were actually used, and the others were decoys that looked like ordinary telephone wires. That would be typical *à la* Spindel.

I checked around further, placing myself in the shoes of Spindel. Where would I hook up the wires inside the house? My research had already shown that the telephone wires and their junction boxes in Marilyn's house today had been changed from the time Marilyn lived there. When Marilyn occupied the house, the wiring came directly from a distant telephone pole to a post attached to the garage. It seemed to me that those old mysterious wires could easily have been hooked up there. If so, Spindel had "bugged" the most sensational murder case ever to be recorded on tape for a client who was the sworn enemy of Robert Kennedy.

Apparently Spindel made several copies of the "Monroe-Kennedy Tapes," as they came to be called by insiders. On one of them could be heard the voices of her murderers. The question was why Hoffa had never made the tapes public. The answer was that he wanted to use them for blackmail.

But in order to fully understand the ins and outs,

several other developments had yet to take place. After that, more of the pieces began to fit, and I began to realize that here was no accidental crossing of people and their schemes; instead, there was a clear pattern.

All the people in the Marilyn Conspiracy were "connected," as if by one of Spindel's wires, but often to see how they "spliced" together I had to go into the archives. I had to use the historian's technique of plowing through musty records to reconstitute the past. In one such document, a transcript of the 1959 McClellan Investigation Committee on Labor Racketeering, I found on page 19828 an official account, characteristic of the relations between Robert Kennedy and "Bernie" Spindel, the following exchange:

Robert Kennedy: I have had some conversation with Mr. Spindel. Mr. Spindel wanted material that we had obtained from him kept confidential . . .

Spindel: That is an absolute lie and he knows that.

Robert Kennedy and Spindel were old adversaries, and the exchange recorded in the transcript interested me because it indicated that Spindel had begun "bugging" Robert Kennedy as early as the beginning of 1959. Spindel dumbfounded the hearing by producing from his briefcase a tape recording of the "conversation" Robert Kennedy referred to. It concerned a secret meeting between Bobby and the wiretapper in a car in the spring of 1959, which "Bernie" had secretly taped. My client learned via Spindel's widow that Robert Kennedy had arranged the hush-hush rendezvous with the Mafia "wireman" in order to get him to desert Hoffa and change sides. Three years later, Spindel secretly recorded in distant Brentwood, California, what has been described by informants as Kennedy-Monroe "pillow talk," as well as the most explosive recording on which is heard the voice of her murderer.

Spindel became Hoffa's "prober" about the time Bobby Kennedy became politically prominent with his vow to "get Hoffa." Through the latter part of the Fifties, Robert Kennedy ws identified with the war on Organized Crime. He fought the Mafia by attacking Hoffa, head of the Brotherhood of Teamsters, as the leading example of mobster control over labor unions. The forum of his battle was the Senate Select Committee on Improper Activities in the Labor Management Field, chaired by Senator McClellan.

From its inception in 1957 through 1960, the McClellan Committee made memorable the names of Bobby Kennedy and Jimmy Hoffa. In those days, the newspaper pictures always showed them in natural opposition, light vs. dark, Camelot vs. the underworld. Throughout the hearings, the intense, combative Committee counsel and the burly, gruff-faced labor racketeer behaved like boxers in a ring. Sharp interrogations and wily evasions did for jabs and dancing maneuvers. The clashes between Bobby and Hoffa during the Senate hearings were soon dubbed "slugfests" by the press.

I recall how shocked everybody was to learn what came out of these sessions. The McClellan Committee revealed the extent to which the underworld had entered mainstream American life. In the case of the Teamsters, mobsters had infiltrated the leadership, their goon squads helping Hoffa become president and overseer of the pension fund of America's richest union. Hoffa put his money at the disposal of the underworld, whose boss of bosses was then Sam "Momo" Giancana, successor to the Chicago syndicate of Al Capone.

Giancana became an important "connection" in our investigation as a link between the Kennedys and Marilyn Monroe. Giancana referred to himself as "boss of bosses" and to John Kennedy as "super-boss." He was the law in the underworld, just as Robert Kennedy was the law in the public world.

During the late Fifties, until Castro's takeover, Giancana's crime network included Cuba, and after the Cuban losses he moved heavily into casinos and vice rackets in Nevada and California through his lieutenant Johnny Roselli. With loans from Hoffa's pension funds, he expanded his Western syndicate, and as Hoffa's close ally, Giancana was subpoenaed to appear before the 1958 McClellan hearings involving the Teamster boss. From his seat, Bobby watched the parade of underworld witnesses, that included Giancana, file before the Senators.

At the time, Bobby kept a journal recently made accessible to Kennedy biographers. In this journal, Bobby noted that the mobsters "wore the same rich clothes, the diamond ring, the jeweled watch, the strong, sickly-sweet smelling perfume."

Among the entries in the red diary, Bob Slatzer had noticed a scribble which he could barely decipher. He asked Marilyn what it meant. She said it referred to Bobby telling her "that he was powerful enough to have people taken care of if they got in his way."

My client had previously heard Marilyn complain of "Bobby's gangster connections." But that seemed unlike the President's younger brother. It rang false to the reputation Robert Kennedy enjoyed of being the government's avenging fury of mobsters and racketeers. When his brother became president in 1961, he appointed Bobby Attorney General. One of the first things the Attorney General did was to create within the Justice Department a special "Get Hoffa Squad" to continue the war on the union leader who so far had been able to avoid being sent to jail. Giancana and Hoffa, in fact, as reported by Kennedy biographers, ranked at the top of Bobby's own "hit list." Bobby Kennedy was known for being a "gangbuster" rather than one who had hired killers in his employ, as Marilyn seemed to imply to Slatzer. And for some time after beginning my investigation, I was uncertain how to tackle this contradiction.

I put the question on the backburner, determined to ignore it until I received definite proof about the fantastic allegations I kept hearing about. A Mafia/ CIA/Kennedy combination over Marilyn's death and the cover-up—that Marilyn Monroe was murdered by some such conspiracy—had been foreshadowed as early as 1964, two years after her death, in a book by Frank Capell, writing that Robert Kennedy was at Marilyn's home when she died. Capell was a self-described "rightwing activist" and rumors similar to those he propagated came out of the L.A. Coroner's office and Police Department, dark hints and secret allegations of either Kennedy, CIA, or underworld involvement in Marilyn's mysterious demise. My best sources early confided that all three were jointly concerned in the affair, but on this point I reserved a doubt. The three were involved but whether jointly, separately, or in opposition was a question that, given their overlapping interests, remained initially unclear. I could go only by the evidence.

My first task in this connection was to ascertain the authenticity of the entries in Marilyn's red diary. If they were correct, it proved that Marilyn had not been "fantasizing." Over the years, all of them turned out to have been remarkable prophecies of things to come. The Bay of Pigs entry was corroborated when Slatzer read about a Florida newspaper publisher who independently confirmed that on the day of the Cuban invasion the President had a backache and left Bobby to run the country. I understood the "S.O.B. Hoffa" entry and its relation to the Spindel bugging of Marilyn's home as having its basis in Marilyn Monroe being close to Bobby. It was Hoffa's logical means of entrapping the Attorney General. I also believed it more than likely that the Kennedy-Monroe tapes, including the "pillow talk" and the accidental pickup of the voices of people present at her death, were still in existence. At this point, however, I was still shuffling bits and pieces; I did not yet see the "big picture." The contradiction remained: "Bobby's gangster connections."

At first, Giancana's and Roselli's significance to the Marilyn Conspiracy was not fully clear. But Slatzer was a pioneer who, despite danger and threats, continued alone for over twelve years his solitary investigation. Norman Mailer, also author of a book on Marilyn, said Slatzer had made it "more difficult to prove Marilyn Monroe took her own life than that she was killed." But Slatzer's could not complete the puzzle until after 1974—the missing pieces were not yet evident. We had as yet failed to substantiate the Mafia connection which would explain Bobby's perplexing references to underworld figures who took care of people "if they got in his way."

Until 1975, I managed an uneasy coexistence with the two Robert Kennedys: the zealous prosecutor of Hoffa and avowed enemy of Organized Crime, and the other of Marilyn's diary, mentioned in the same breath with the name of the "boss of bosses." But this contradiction disappeared piece by piece through the summer and fall of 1975 as I followed the sensational revelations coming out of the Senate Intelligence Committee investigation of CIA-Mafia activities during the early Kennedy years.

The Senate disclosures showed that there had been intimate relations between the underworld and the government in the Kennedy period. These relations were not static. They varied according to circumstances. There had been a willingness on both sides to "deal." The pursued and pursuer at times made a truce. For self-interest, the enemies would work together. Looked at this way, it can be understood that the Attorney General, scourge of "sickly-sweet smelling" underworld dragoons, might very well have "gangster connections," even such as "Giancana" and "Roselli"—the same names my client had seen in the red diary.

In my profession, "shock" is a luxury I cannot afford. But I admit sharing this reaction with many Americans after the 1975 Senate disclosures of underworld involvement in the Kennedy presidency. The Committee set off the biggest bombshell when it found in the CIA files the name of a woman who had been simultaneously the girl friend of President Kennedy and Mafia boss Giancana. When her name was revealed, the woman called a press conference and confirmed her relationship with both men. She admitted visiting the President at the White House nearly two dozen times while she was Giancana's mistress. She said she and the President were introduced in Las Vegas by Frank Sinatra, and that Sinatra had later introduced her to Giancana, who in turn had introduced her to Johnny Roselli.

The names of Giancana and Roselli had previously surfaced in the hearings when an astonishing CIA-Mafia plot to overthrow Castro was disclosed. In 1961, government agents contacted Johnny Roselli, who brought in Giancana, an associate of Havana's pre-Castro Mafia boss. In Cuba, the Kennedys wanted to topple the Communist government and mobsters wanted to recover the Havana vice rackets. A deal was struck. The CIA enlisted Giancana and Roselli to kill the Cuban leader.

According to the authors of the recent best-seller *The Kennedys,* Robert Kennedy ran the Cuban operation out of the Attorney General's office after being appointed by his brother overseer of anti-Castro activities. The secret CIA war against Cuba, called Operation Mongoose, was Bobby's personal creation. The authors report that as early as May 1961, the Attorney General knew about CIA murder plots involving hired killers, and that a year later the CIA brass gave him a full briefing on the Mafia part in the operation. This briefing took place around the time Bobby began his serious romance with Marilyn Monroe. It explains Marilyn's entries in the red diary concerning Giancana, Roselli, the Bay of Pigs, Cuba, and her telling my client about "Bobby's gangster connections."

In my investigation, what mattered was that the entries Marilyn made in 1962 were borne out by a government committee. The information in her diary could have come only from Robert Kennedy, whom she was seeing during the time he waged the secret CIA war. The Committee had made mention of the assassination of President Raphael Trujillo of the Dominican Republic; Robert Kennedy had also told Marilyn about this. President Diem, as Marilyn noted

Bobby saying, never received sanctuary in the United States. The Committee findings indicated that Bobby indeed had been in command of the Bay of Pigs, as he had told Marilyn. And with Giancana and Roselli participating in Operation Mongoose, Robert Kennedy had the "gangster connections" of which Marilyn expressed fear to Bob Slatzer.

Before Senator Church could question Giancana, he was found murdered in his Oak Hill, Illinois, home. A few months later, before he could be questioned, Johnny Roselli was also found murdered, floating in a barrel in Biscayne Bay, off the Miami coast. Following these events, the Committee rapidly wound down, the chairman denying until the end that there was evidence of an "underworld-Kennedy link."

I learned an invaluable lesson in politics and its principle of opportunism by following the hearings. They made clear that the contradiction which long had stumped me had been nonexistent.

The Robert Kennedy of the "Get Hoffa Squad" and the Robert Kennedy of Operation mongoose were one and the same person, a person who covered both sides of the street. Bobby thought he could play fast and loose with the flashy, rough-spoken members of the mob. He thought that a Harvard boy was a match for criminals wearing diamond rings and jeweled watches. He believed that with college smarts he could outfox the wily mobsters, seeking to place them behind bars while at the same time using them to do a "dirty job" in Cuba. But he underestimated his opponents. Perhaps, like Marilyn, with all his boyish calculation, he also was too "vulnerable."

About three weeks before her death, Bobby cut off his relations with Marilyn, changing his private number and refusing to accept her calls at the Justice

Department. Marilyn had become unreliable. She had information that could kill the Kennedys politically, perhaps even bring impeachment to his brother. He had become aware of how dangerously both he and his brother were entangled with the mob. The syndicate had a hold over the White House. They could blackmail the President of the United States.

The world of the Mafia, the CIA, the two Kennedy brothers, and Marilyn Monroe overlapped. The situation seemed complex, but in it all the characters connected. This was something I saw clearly while following Marilyn's path through the same world that involved Giancana and the Kennedys. In the West, the two Mafia territories were Hollywood and Las Vegas, and Marilyn lived in one and spent much time in the other through her longstanding romance with Frank Sinatra.

Sinatra was another of the unattainable men in Marilyn's life. She told Bob Slatzer, who was then gathering information for a biography on her, that Frank Sinatra was the "most fascinating man" she had ever dated. To her maid, she confessed he was the "sexiest" man in the world. Until nearly the end of her life, Marilyn hoped that she and Sinatra would marry.

Marilyn met Sinatra in the early Fifties and began a relationship with him after her divorce from DiMaggio that lasted until her death. During the last two years of her life, following the breakup of the marriage to Miller, a time when her mental disintegration became marked, she and Sinatra were frequent companions on his yacht, at his house in Palm Springs, in Las Vegas and at the Cal-Neva Lodge, a casino on the California-Nevada state line in which Sinatra's business interests were combined with the likes of Sam "Momo" Giancana. The famous crooner often performed there while hosting celebrities and political prominents, including Marilyn Monroe and members of the Kennedy clan. The Cal-Neva Lodge embroiled Frank Sinatra with the shadowy figures of the underworld. When he gave Marilyn a poodle, she humorously named it "Maf," short for "Mafia," a name to which Sinatra reportedly objected.

Marilyn Monroe moved through many different worlds and one of them was the underworld. When as an unknown starlet she first met Joe Schenck, one of the founders of Twentieth Century–Fox, he had just finished serving a jail sentence for making Mafia payoffs to Johnny Roselli. According to one recent investigator, Marilyn Monroe and Roselli dated in the early Fifties when Roselli was already Giancana's man in the West. Hollywood oldtimers know that Harry Cohn, who gave Marilyn her first talking role, obtained control of Columbia Pictures through mob money provided by Roselli.

Marilyn's underworld connections came with the terrain of Hollywood and Las Vegas. It was the same world known to Jack and Bobby Kennedy through their friendship with Peter Lawford and Frank Sinatra. The two worlds traded commodities with each other—one provided killers, the other, women. One of those women was Marilyn Monroe, and she became a pawn played off by one world against the other.

At the time of Bobby's affair with Marilyn, Jimmy Hoffa was finally indicted for extortion. Sam Giancana was to be prosecuted in a wiretapping case. But during Bobby's attorney generalship, Hoffa was never put in jail. The charges against Giancana were dropped. The Mafia participation in the CIA's Cuban adventures did not cease until 1963.

A deal had been struck with Marilyn as the "chip." The chip was expendable. Someone came in the night of August 4th and gave her an injection.

Who that person was we shall probably never know, but we do know that Marilyn was an unstable woman with important secrets. And that when she died, the death was made to look like a suicide.

A cover-up was directed from the highest levels in order to protect interests that converged on the barbiturate-craving body and disintegrating mind of Marilyn Monroe.

Sometimes Bob Slatzer used to argue with Marilyn about the time and money she wasted on psychiatrists. Marilyn admitted that she lied to them. She seemed to think it funny that through that costly hour in which the soul is disrobed, she kept hers clothed in "fantasies." On the couch she "fantasized" to the quiet listener. Beyond a certain point in self-revelation, she said, she could not go.

Not long before her death, she told my client, "I've always had a slight superstition about insanity. It's said to run in my family." Marilyn's mother, Gladys Monroe Mortenson, had been placed in an "insane asylum" when her daughter was less than a year old. Marilyn's maternal grandmother, married to Otis Elmer Monroe, was throughout her life committed by the courts to mental institutions; she died in a state hospital in 1927, a year after Marilyn's birth.

In February 1961, shortly after her divorce from Arthur Miller, Marilyn was committed to the Payne Whitney Psychiatric Clinic in New York City. She was put on the "dangerous floor" in a locked cell with an observation window through which doctors stared at her. The two most influential people in her life during the four years she lived in New York were her psychiatrist, Dr. Marianne Kris, and her acting coaches Paula and Lee Strasberg. Marilyn was attending the Strasbergs' famous Actors Studio and studying "method acting" to become a "serious actress."

I was able to see a letter which Marilyn wrote from her locked cell. "Dr. Kris has put me into the hospital," it reads. "Please help me, Lee. This is the *last* place I should be—maybe if you call Dr. Kris and assure her of my sensitivity and that I must get back to class so I'll be better prepared . . ."

From her locked cell, Marilyn sent out a pathetic cry, but the influential people in her life failed her. A year-and-a-half later, in the bedroom in her house in Brentwood, again the "influential people" did not intervene.

In critical periods of her life, Marilyn's second husband, Joe DiMaggio, stepped in and managed to set things right. He was able to get her out of Payne Whitney, but he could not stop the events that followed. After her death, DiMaggio remained unforgiving of Bobby Kennedy. The baseball hero knew Marilyn's vulnerability, and that behind the stunning beauty she was fragile; the sex symbol easily broke.

Dr. Greenson said that he had tried to wean Marilyn from drugs but had "failed." Columnist Walter Winchell, with whom Bob Slatzer communicated through the years, wrote darkly in his column that the night Marilyn died a top Washington VIP had "failed" her.

Chapter Six

THE D.A.

Bernard Spindel, while working for Jimmy Hoffa, had made a tape recording the night of Marilyn's death on which could be heard the sound of a slap followed by the sound of a body striking the ground, and someone asking, "What shall we do with the body?"

After investigating the Marilyn mystery for nearly a decade, I no longer thought it an easy job to convince the world that Marilyn Monroe did not commit suicide. I almost despaired of getting the authorities with the power to reopen an investigation over to my side. But with the approach of the twentieth anniversary of Marilyn's death, things took a sudden turn.

In early August 1982, I co-authored a five-page story, "Who Killed Marilyn Monroe?" The story appeared in *US* magazine and coincided with my widely publicized news conference. Each event created a sensation. It brought home to me that the world had not forgotten Marilyn Monroe, nor the circumstances under which she died. The public's fascination with Marilyn Monroe continues today, and I discovered that the same doubts which had prompted my investigation into her death were still current among many people.

Before the news conference I had advance releases printed and circulated, advising that I would brief the media and answer all questions at the greater Los Angeles Press Club at nine o'clock on the morning of August 4. Meanwhile, as the result of the *US* article, a groundswell had built and my phone began to ring off the hook. One call a few days before the news conference was from a reporter with the Los Angeles *Herald Examiner,* who said he was writing a piece on L.A. County Coroner Dr. Thomas Noguchi. He asked for my comments and a "few quotes."

I was about to tell him that everyone I knew was writing a piece on Noguchi. Dr. Noguchi was "Coroner to the Stars," known nationally for his autopsies on Hollywood celebrities and in Los Angeles for his battles with the County Board of Supervisors, who for years had tried to remove him from office, demote him, or get rid of him in other ways. Dr. Noguchi had performed autopsies on stars like Janis Joplin, Sharon Tate, Natalie Wood, William Holden and John Belushi. He did the autopsy on Bobby Kennedy after his 1969 assassination in Los Angeles. But his first famous case was Marilyn Monroe back in 1962; Dr. Noguchi then was still a deputy medical examiner.

The Coroner's report and the handling of Marilyn's autopsy were from the very beginning a focal point of my investigation. I believed that the autopsy had been improperly assessed as a "probable suicide." Dr. Noguchi, going by that assumption, performed his examination accordingly. I described Dr. Noguchi's report as "incomplete" to the newsman. When Dr. Noguchi got Marilyn's body, the doctors at the death scene had already decided that she had killed herself by "overdose," which immediately afterwards became the official verdict issued by County Coroner Curphey. I then passed on to other topics related to the "cover-up," making brief mention of the red diary and the reward we'd offered for its recovery.

The day before the news conference I was handed a copy of the *Herald Examiner* and realized that I'd made the front page. My quote about Dr. Noguchi never made the edition. Perhaps my criticism of the coroner's report was not nearly so interesting as the disappearance of Marilyn's personal documents. "Big Reward Offered for Marilyn's Lost Diary," the headline read. The wire services picked it up from the *Herald Examiner*, and in the following weeks the missing diary remained a prime story.

At the news conference, a packed media audience clamored to hear more about the red diary, but I fended off the requests; it had received sufficient notice, I felt, and there was more direct evidence that Marilyn Monroe had been murdered. This had been murmured for over twenty years. But not until 1982, when I demanded an official investigation by the D.A., had it been so emphatically stated.

I learned the pitfalls of public attention. In the days following the news conference, much of my time was consumed calling up wire agencies and news stations to correct being misquoted. Like my Noguchi interview which resulted in headlines about the red diary, my news conference produced the headline, "CIA Killed Marilyn, Detective Claims." The editors who heard my complaints offered the apology that sometimes a quote will be shortened. Meanwhile my "shortened quote" created lengthy confusion. At the news conference, my answer to the question from one of the press corps had been wrenched from the body of my reply. To the question, "Who killed Marilyn Monroe?" I'd replied, "Perhaps a dissident-type faction, a CIA-type group."

The media played up this part, instead of seeking a fuller explanation of the term "dissident-type faction." But to have given a clearer notion of what I meant would have involved discussing the even more controversial CIA tie-in with the underworld. That would have compelled me to explain the Mafia role in Marilyn's death. Such a discussion would have been premature.

To have gone into complex issues at this early stage would have merely turned me into the mouthpiece for another "conspiracy theory." My immediate aim was to prod the L.A. County Board of Supervisors and the District Attorney into reopening an investigation. To make the case stick, a murder charge would have to be proven. That was the legal requirement to convene a Grand Jury, as the Statute of Limitations for any impropriety involved in the Marilyn cover-up, whether proved or not, had expired. The single exception was murder. I did not doubt that the results of an investigation would lead the D.A. to demand a formal inquest by the Grand Jury. My only concern was that the task was not being taken seriously enough. District Attorney Van de Kamp called it a "threshold investigation."

In my opinion, that was a mistake. Only a full probe could lay to rest a matter that had haunted the office of the D.A. for over twenty years. In fact, the "cover-up" might be said to have begun back in 1962 when the

D.A., glancing over the Coroner's report, believed the case to be closed. In any event, I saw quite a few surprised faces in 1974 when Bob Slatzer and I first petitioned the L.A. County Grand Jury for an official investigation. We came armed with massive evidence, the result of my client's twelve-year study. Not long afterward, we received from the Foreman of the Grand Jury a one-paragraph letter stating that the case did not merit being reopened.

Since the Grand Jury changes from year to year, we thought we'd wait till 1975—but in 1975 we had no better luck. The original investigators were said to be "competent and complete" in their findings. In 1975 we had even more information, but the Grand Jury would not even review the case, much less reopen it.

At this point, we were in a quandary. Whom could we turn to? One other alternative was left. We could direct a demand to Dr. Noguchi at the Coroner's office. But just then, Dr. Noguchi was under a cloud. He had recently gone before the Civil Service Commission and won reinstatement to the job from which the Board of Supervisors had tried to oust him. The hearings before the Commission had been rife with macabre testimonies. For years, Dr. Noguchi had been criticized by medical authorities for the way he had handled the Marilyn Monroe case. But the great opportunity to question him more closely on the subject was lost in their zeal for character assassination. Los Angeles was entertained by bizarre statements from witnesses who claimed Dr. Noguchi prayed for air crashes in the city or that he rubbed his hands with satisfaction when he saw gurneys stacked with dead bodies at the county morgue. The Civil Service Commission had awarded Dr. Noguchi his job back, and on our part it would have been naive to think that the Coroner was about to jeopardize his hard-won reinstatement by rocking the boat anew with a review of his most controversial autopsy.

In 1975, there was one more door on which we could knock. We could go to the L.A. County District Attorney. But our knocking, we soon discovered, was unwelcome there. The D.A. literally told my client, "It's a closed door."

However, seven years later, following my news conference, I was to receive a pleasant surprise. Picking up the newspaper, I learned that the Board of Supervisors had unanimously voted to request District Attorney John Van de Kamp to open the Marilyn case for investigation. At last, Bob Slatzer and I had a taste of victory. The County, with its greater resources, would do justice to our long years of probing. Two decades after Marilyn's death, the full story might at last come out.

Although Van de Kamp had accepted the request to reopen the case, in his formal announcement he called it a "review." I was not well pleased with the wording, and preferred that he rightly call it an "investigation." But at the very least, the D.A. admitted that he was undertaking the inquiry since back in 1962 "there had been no investigation."

Basically, the D.A.'s job was to put together and analyze the circumstances of Marilyn's death. I planned to watch the proceedings closely. If the D.A. was serious about his "review," he would have to ask the following questions:

• Where was Marilyn's housekeeper, Mrs. Eunice Murray, on the afternoon of August 4, 1962?

In her first statement to the police and the press,

Mrs. Murray had affirmed that she had not left the house but had stayed on through the night, and was the first to discover Marilyn's body. She also had denied that Robert Kennedy visited Marilyn's house late that afternoon, because she said she would have seen him. Mrs. Murray might also be asked why she was running the washer and dryer when Sgt. Clemmons arrived at the house, what were the contents of the boxes Clemmons saw her load into the car, or why she called her handyman son-in-law, Norman Jeffries II, to come over and repair a bedroom window before the police arrived.

• Who was present at Marilyn's house in the early morning hours of August 5, 1962, before the police were called?

By the advanced state of rigor mortis and bodily discoloration observed by Clemmons and the mortician Hockett, Marilyn had died at approximately 8:00 to 8:30 P.M. on August 4 and not about 12:30 in the early hour of the following morning as Mrs. Murray first stated. Marilyn had been dead about eight hours, not the "three hours" claimed by the two doctors present, Greenson and Engelberg. Pat Newcomb, in one of the few interviews she has ever given on Marilyn, told my client that she received a call from Marilyn's lawyer, "Mickey" Rudin, Dr. Greenson's brother-in-law, about 4:00 A.M. the morning of August 5, thirty minutes before the police were notified. She said Rudin called her from Marilyn's home.

• Where was Bobby Kennedy in the twenty-four hours preceding Marilyn's death?

According to police and FBI reports verified by Sgt. Jack Clemmons and the hotel desk at San Francisco's St. Francis Hotel, Robert Kennedy was there

August 3. Police records also indicate that during the late hours of that same day, Bobby Kennedy was listed as having checked into the Beverly Hilton Hotel in Los Angeles. He checked out about noon on August 4 and went to Peter Lawford's house.

• What was Peter Lawford's role and where was he during the early hours of August 5?

Lawford's former wife says he went to Marilyn's house to "clean up" before the police arrived. Police records reveal that he was at Marilyn's house with Bobby Kennedy in the afternoon of August 4.

• Who was the man seen entering Marilyn's house with Bobby about 5:00 P.M.?

Marilyn's neighbors told my client that the man was carrying a "doctor's bag."

• Where are Marilyn's telephone records?

Less than twenty-four hours before she died, Marilyn had told Slatzer that she was planning to hold a news conference on Monday morning, August 6, if Bobby Kennedy refused to answer the telephone calls she had placed to him "through the switchboard at the Justice Department." That same Monday morning, two men confiscated Marilyn's log from the General Telephone Company in Brentwood. The late L.A. Police Chief William H. Parker was the last person known to have them in this possession.

• What was the role of the Suicide Investigation Team in the "official" investigation of Marilyn's death?

Normally, in a case as suspicious as Marilyn's demise, the Coroner holds an inquest. Instead, Dr. Theodore Curphey, then L.A. County Coroner, appointed a "Suicide Investigation Team" consisting of two doctors who were to question "those persons close to Marilyn in the last days before her death." Their report agreed with Dr. Curphey's verdict of "probable suicide."

Shortly after making my pitch to the District Attorney at the L.A. Press Club, I spoke by telephone with the Assistant District Attorney, Ronald M. "Mike" Carroll.

"Milo," Carroll asked, "did you get hold of the tapes?" He was referring to the clandestine "Kennedy-Monroe" tapes made at Marilyn's home, said to have accidentally recorded the sounds of the murder.

I then knew that the Assistant D.A. was already familiar with my client's work on the Spindel operation.

"Not yet," I answered, adding cryptically, "but speaking of tapes, do you have an audio cassette tape recorder in your office?"

Carroll said he didn't, but promised to have one ready for our meeting in his office the following day.

Although I hadn't as yet met the man in charge of the official "review," our names had been recently linked in newspaper articles. I did not doubt that he had run a check on me, and I reciprocated the courtesy. It might seem superfluous to check out a man who held a position as responsible as Carroll's, second only to the District Attorney. In my business, however, regardless of the office a person holds, it's a thing I do routinely.

Prior to our meeting, we agreed that it be kept "secret." Perhaps the fact that I had told people from his office that I was writing a book made the D.A. apprehensive. Carroll, probably aware that media people hounded me for interviews, asked me not to disclose anything about our meeting. He came down very hard on that point.

Giving him my word that I would not "go public," I tried to assure him that I was not a "headline-hunter." I explained that I was an investigator as well as an author, and when I set out for his office the next day, my briefcase held a copy of my latest book, *How to Protect Your Life and Property*. I wanted to draw his attention to the chapter called "Mr. District Attorney," in which I deal with the types of evidence required for conviction. As an example, I cite a murder committed twenty years ago, evaluating its chances of being brought to trial as practically nil. I hoped Carroll would read this. I wanted him to realize what we were up against. We had to get evidence that was "one hundred percent proof" in order to go to trial.

When I entered the stone portals of the L.A. Criminal Courts building downtown, I was surprised to see that the directory still listed Dr. Noguchi as County Coroner. I thought it strange because at that time the Board of Supervisors actually had succeeded in demoting him. It was all over the papers. Dr. Noguchi was the genuine article when it came to "newsmakers." People were fascinated by the "Coroner to the Stars." Marilyn Monroe was his first autopsy on a famous person, and I felt he'd been given a raw deal for being made responsible for inadequacies in the way it was handled. Dr. Noguchi shared the same building with the team that was to investigate him and the conduct of the Coroner's office twenty years ago.

On that day in September, the downtown temperature stood at 95 degrees. It was hot and smoggy. The short walk from the parking lot was suffocating, and gratefully I recovered in the elevator that took me to Mike Carroll's office on the eighteenth floor.

After I got out of the elevator, a few abrupt turnings

of the corridor would take me to the press room I'd often visited before, where media people worked the County beat. In this particular instance, however, I entered what turned out to be the most guarded floor in the whole building. It had a reception area where I announced myself to a man in uniform. Moments later, I was greeted by Al Tomich, special investigator with D.A.'s division and chief investigator assigned to the Monroe case. Tomich took me to the office of Mike Carroll, where I met the Assistant D.A. and Clayton Anderson, the other investigator.

Carroll, Tomich and Anderson were the triumvirate in charge of the Monroe "review." They looked upright and incorruptible. Their craggy faces seemed to have the bulldog quality, the tenacity, the will to see it through to the end. Time would tell. Meanwhile, I held them spellbound by withdrawing a cassette from a manila envelope.

"Gentlemen," I said, "the tape runs about fifteen minutes."

The craggy faces stared intently. The little cassette hypnotized them. I admit I enjoy these moments of drama. I suppose every detective, bogged down in paperwork, shares a similar feeling when given the chance to demonstrate results.

The tape recorder I had requested was on Carroll's desk. I handed the tape to Tomich. I was seated directly in front of Carroll. Tomich was also seated directly in front of Carroll. Tomich was to my left, Clayton to my right. I explained the tape's origin, but left them in the dark as to what they were about to hear. It was necessary that I tell them that no law would be broken by recording or playing the tape. It held pertinent information regarding Marilyn's murder, legally obtained, though by a highly unusual method.

Tomich closed the lid and pushed the play button. Static crackled through the room as the leader of the tape passed through. The triumvirate looked on in silence. The crackling continued; one of the men coughed the way people cough when they wish to express skepticism. Whichever of the three it was, I could assure him that momentarily a voice would break the silence, a voice I'd heard and studied many times. In the quiet evening hour in my office, I had listened by the single light of my desk lamp, playing the tape again and again, then locking the cassette back into the vault, the voice with its powerful confession accompanying me to my car to fill the silence as I drove home.

In spots the tape was poor and occasionally unintelligible. But where it was clear, the voice of an informant was heard. Even I, long familiar with the information, felt shock upon hearing the coldblooded business it described. The triumvirate listened with the same look of intense preoccupation. They heard the informant identify himself as a former associate of Bernard Spindel and of a man I will call "D.C." He stated that Bernard Spindel, while working for Jimmy Hoffa, had made a tape recording the night of Marilyn's death on which could be heard the sound of a slap followed by the sound of a body striking the ground, and someone asking, "What shall we do with the body?"

The informant mentioned the names of those that could be heard on the Spindel/Hoffa tape, but all of us who share this knowledge have agreed to keep it secret. I cannot reveal the name of the man I call "D.C.," though it may be found in the directory of the Watergate, the building complex off Capitol Hill notorious for its "plumbers." Without the actual Spindel/

Hoffa tape it would be unethical to reveal the identities involved in this tape. The tape recording I played was itself not evidence, as both Carroll and I were well aware. It was "information." Though I considered it coming from an unimpeachable source, the tape did not meet the rules of admissibility, even if I had additional documentation to back it up. The voice on the tape stated that one of the two men present in Marilyn's house the night she died was a well-known star of motion pictures. The other was a high-ranking political appointee.

But to get a verdict of murder twenty years after the fact is almost impossible. It requires absolute proof. In the Monroe case, virtually nothing short of a confession could get the D.A.'s office to recommend further investigation, or to turn it over to the L.A. County Grand Jury. Although this might be impossible under the circumstances, I would be satisfied to see the cover-up exposed. I wondered how far Carroll's men were prepared to go. If they went the full route, there'd be a scandal. If they thoroughly beat the bushes, they were bound to find the killer. Tomich had me worried with his sharp repetition of the injunction laid on me by Deputy D.A. Carroll, "We're not giving anything to the press."

The D.A. team covered most of the specific allegations connected with the foul play and the cover-up I believed to be involved in Marilyn's death. It addressed itself to the activities of Mrs. Murray on August 4, 1962, the conduct of the Coroner's office, the red diary, Lionel Grandison's signature on the death certificate, Marilyn's vanished telephone toll records for the period near her death, the Miner Memorandum, the Spindel operation, Bobby Kennedy's whereabouts the weekend of August 3–5, and Sgt. Clemmons' criticism of the death scene investigation.

The investigators examined all these matters, and in the end answered my question about their "bulldog quality." In December 1982, the District Attorney reported its conclusion that based "on the information available, no further criminal investigation appears required into Miss Monroe's death."

For a long time, any murder theory involving Marilyn eventually came up against the testimony of three people who were the last to see her alive: Mrs. Eunice Murray, the housekeeper; Pat Newcomb, the public relations girl known in Hollywood as a "handler," and Dr. Greenson, the psychiatrist. All three, together and separately, were with Marilyn at various times throughout much of the day and early evening of August 4, but from the very beginning, their testimony has shown a mass of contradictions. They contradict each other. They change their recollections, and they contradict themselves. It's always been my feeling that the confusion they created was a deliberate attempt to obscure the facts of what happened when Marilyn died.

Their inconsistencies are on a par with the inconsistencies of others, particularly those of Peter Lawford, who never stopped adding to the confusion and took with him to the grave the secret of Marilyn's final hours when he died in 1984. The widespread confusion surrounding Marilyn's death, and the glaring discrepancies in testimony, should have tipped off the District Attorney back in 1962, as it should have alerted the District Attorney twenty years later. And I wondered if it was mere coincidence that two D.A.'s, two decades apart, in the case of one vital document, the "Miner Memorandum," seemed to be equally careless of its implications. This document is important to the "cover-up" for a number of reasons. It shows that from the very beginning the Office of the District Attorney was given notice of a disagreement with Chief County Coroner Curphey, who was in charge of the Marilyn autopsy.

In 1962, the Miner Memorandum had been filed away and forgotten. In 1982, the D.A. review into the death of Marilyn Monroe reported that a "thorough search was made of all District Attorney's records in order to secure the Miner Memorandum. It was not found." To learn what this document contained, the D.A.'s investigators had to re-interview the author who was then, twenty years later, in private practice in Los Angeles. But bound by professional ethics and an oath sworn to Dr. Greenson in 1962, he refused to tell the investigators any more than he had noted in the interoffice memorandum he had sent at that time, in which he had outlined his personal belief that "Miss Monroe had not committed suicide."

At the time this explosive memorandum came to be written its author, John Miner, had the title of Deputy District Attorney. He was also the District Attorney's Legal-Medical Head. With a keen interest in medical matters, he was subsequently to specialize in medical-legal prosecutions. John Miner often witnessed autopsies in the Coroner's Office, and on the morning of August 5 he had watched Dr. Noguchi perform the autopsy on Marilyn Monroe. Within that same week, he had personally interviewed Dr. Ralph Greenson. According to the 1982 investigators who spoke with Miner, he "had felt compelled to express his reservations to the Chief Deputy District Attorney, Dr. Curphey and others."

With this reservation of its own Legal-Medical Head, the D.A. should have instructed the County Coroner to hold an inquest, which in the case of a homicide follows a procedure far more thorough than the regular autopsy such as that performed by Dr. Noguchi on Marilyn Monroe, where no homicide was suspected. John Miner attended Noguchi's autopsy and his observations, according to the 1982 D.A. report, "support Dr. Noguchi's physical findings." Yet when writing the memorandum about Marilyn Monroe's suicide, he included Dr. Noguchi's superior, Dr. Theodore Curphey, as he might have been aware of the need for an inquest.

The 1982 D.A. report in its conclusion discounted that Marilyn was murdered by reasoning that her murder would have required a "massive, in-place conspiracy." But in my experience that's rarely the case. A "cover-up" is usually a more subtle process. It may begin with nothing more "conspiratorial" than a higher-up repeating to a clerk a message he has just received, "About that Miner Memorandum. File it somewhere. We've got more important things to worry about." And so it is filed, and a few years later a different employee with the instruction, "Destroy everything dated August 1962," sets the file in order. Knowing as I do the ways of government, I think that's been the likely fate of the Miner Memorandum.

District Attorney John Van de Kamp's report dismissed the Miner Memorandum "as a footnote to our inquiries." I have always felt the D.A. did not go far enough. He quit the field too soon. Dr. Greenson by then had passed away, and could no longer be questioned. But enough is known from the contradictory

Marilyn, on the left, at age seven, with a friend. From her family album.

Marilyn, fifteen years old and in high school.

During the war, Marilyn worked in an aircraft factory and practiced modeling poses on weekends.

Marilyn's first wedding, to Jim Dougherty.

One of Marilyn's first professional swimsuit sessions, on
Malibu Beach in 1949.

A 1950 pin-up shot and, opposite, a 1951 pose.

In the year that passed between these two photo sessions, Marilyn established her famous "look."

Marilyn in one of her earliest films, *Ladies of the Chorus*.

In the 1952 release *Niagara*, Marilyn was finally a "star."

Marilyn reviews a "mug shot" book of herself, fine tuning her dramatic expressions.

Marilyn with her first drama coach, Natasha Lytess.

Makeup man
Whitey Snyder
preparing the star
for *Gentlemen
Prefer Blondes*.

A despondent
Marilyn on the set
of *Something's Got
to Give* (1962), her
final, uncompleted,
film.

Undressing for a scene in *Something's Got to Give*.

Rare photo of Dr. Ralph Greenson, Marilyn's psychiatrist.

Dr. Hyman Engelberg, Marilyn's internist.

Frank Sinatra and Peter Lawford, two of Marilyn's closest friends in Hollywood. Both failed her.

Pat Newcomb, Marilyn's Press Agent and "handler."

Marilyn with third husband, Joe DiMaggio.

Bob Slatzer with Marilyn in Hollywood.

Sgt. Jack Clemmons, the first detective on the scene the night the actress died.

Lionel Grandison, the deputy coroner's aide who was forced to sign Marilyn's death certificate.

With her dog "Maf," short for Mafia, a gift from Frank Sinatra.

Peter Lawford's Santa Monica beach house, where Marilyn and Bobby Kennedy secretly met.

Slatzer at Marilyn's Brentwood bungalow.

With her co-stars on the set of *The Misfits*, 1960.

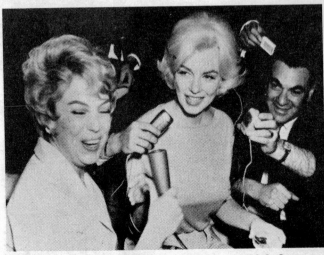

Marilyn's last press conference in 1962, a month before she died. The next one was scheduled for the Monday after her death.

Walter Schaefer, head of the ambulance service that picked up Marilyn, still alive, on August 4th.

Mrs. Eunice Murray, Marilyn's housekeeper, who, 25 years after Monroe's death, finally talked.

Marilyn on the set of *Something's Got to Give*. Her career was faltering, but the magic was still there.

A policeman points to the jumble of drug bottles on Marilyn's bedside table. If she swallowed enough of these pills to kill her, why weren't any traces of them found in her stomach? (AP/WIDE WORLD PHOTO)

Marilyn's bedroom, photographed the day after she died. She was found naked on the bed, the satin coverlet tangled around her feet. The door on the left leads to the bathroom; the open door, on the right, leads to the hall. Marilyn's housekeeper recently changed her testimony about what she saw under this door the night Marilyn died. (UPI/BETTMANN NEWSPHOTOS)

statements about Marilyn's state of mind the psychiatrist expressed to Dr. Curphey's Suicide Investigation Team and remarks on the same subject made to John Miner to leave us in doubt. Back in 1962, this conflicting testimony should have "flagged" the D.A. Why was the document "buried" and destroyed?

Miner interviewed Greenson a few days after Marilyn's death. To the Suicide Investigation Team, Dr. Greenson maintained that his patient, "despondent" and unable to accept "rejection," had killed herself. But to Miner, the D.A.'s Legal-Medical Head, he stated that prior to her death "Miss Monroe appeared to be making progress, on a psychiatric level," and that she had been making plans for her future. Dr. Greenson presented a "psychological profile" of Marilyn Monroe inconsistent with suicide, which Miner accepted. The 1982 D.A. report concluded from its talks with Miner that, based on his conversations with Dr. Greenson, he believed that "in terms of a psychological profile, Marilyn Monroe did not commit an intentional act of suicide," and that he disagreed with the act of self-destruction, "as proffered by the Suicide Investigation Team."

Greenson apparently confided to Miner things which he did not tell anyone else. No one, as far as I know, has ever heard the "Greenson tapes" except Miner. These could be as valuable as the Hoffa/Spindel tapes in determining what troubled Marilyn before she died, and so establish the possible motive for her murder. But back in 1962, the psychiatrist bound Miner to secrecy. "During Miner's extensive interview with Greenson," the D.A. reports, "Miner agreed that he would not repeat to anyone the details of Marilyn Monroe's statements and tape recordings given to Greenson during their therapy sessions."

It is believed that Dr. Greenson destroyed the tapes before he died. Until his death in 1979, he seemed to have carried the burden of an anguished knowledge. At times, he seemed exasperated because there were things he wanted to reveal but couldn't. He might have told John Miner, but John Miner gave his word and has never broken it.

Eunice Murray, Marilyn's housekeeper, raised the suspicion of Sgt. Clemmons, the weekend Watch Commander at the Santa Monica Police Station who was first to arrive upon the death scene at Helena Drive. His suspicions were soon shared by my client, as well as myself, and ultimately by all who have written about the curious end of Marilyn Monroe. The original account Mrs. Murray gave to the Los Angeles Police Department changed as time went by. Finally, she was to make an astounding admission, but not until 1985, after nearly a quarter century had passed. Perhaps she was like those many others I ran up against in my investigation. A lot of people were still scared to testify as to what went on around the time Marilyn died. Mrs. Murray was the last person to see Marilyn alive. She looked "scared," noted the police sergeant when he came to the death scene.

Bob Slatzer's suspicions of the housekeeper were roused when he saw in the police report her testimony that the "light under Marilyn's closed door" caused her to become alarmed and call Dr. Greenson. Slatzer knew that it couldn't have been. He happened to be familiar with the thick white wool carpeting that Marilyn had put in her house. It came from India and had a thick pad underneath. Marilyn had difficulty opening and closing the door, as the nap of the white wool carpeting caused friction. When she showed this to Slatzer less than a month before she died, he advised her that she was going to ruin the expensive floor covering by wearing off the nap. He suggested that the handyman trim the bottoms of the doors so they could close without trouble.

When Slatzer interviewed Mrs. Murray in 1973, he brought up the "light under the door." Mrs. Murray now stated that it was the telephone cord which had led to Marilyn's bedroom. After Slatzer's interview, she wrote in her memoirs about the new white wool carpet that filled the space under the door: "The surface wool had piled up as a result of contact with the swinging door. This I remembered later, but not until after I agreed that I had seen a light under the door. Such are the pitfalls of demands under pressure when accurate reporting is desired." She added, "The telephone cord led to Marilyn's bedroom, but there was no sound of conversation within." When my client related this to Walter Winchell, the dean of columnists sighed laconically, "Strange, how people's stories change when they have time to think things over."

My client disbelieved Mrs. Murray's humble position in Marilyn's household from the very beginning. Ostensibly, she was housekeeper, but in her memoirs she alluded to people she'd worked with, "some seriously ill with depression or schizophrenia, while others, like Marilyn Monroe, were merely recovering from stressful experiences and needed supportive aid to establish life along more structured lines." Mrs. Murray stated that she was qualified to assist under a psychiatrist's guidance "in any kind of therapy that seemed indicated."

Whatever her official position, Mrs. Murray projected in Marilyn's home the influence of Dr. Greenson, an influence already pervasive, on a round-the-clock basis. About one year after starting treatment, Dr. Greenson made the unprecedented decision to move Marilyn's therapy from his office to his home, a decision which was to cause a minor flap in medical circles when it was revealed after Marilyn's death, since it violated the psychiatric canon of doctor-patient separation. Sometimes they had three sessions daily, occasionally at least one session every day of the week. Marilyn frequently stayed over at the Greensons', becoming virtually a part of the family that included the psychiatrist's wife, his college-age son and daughter, as well as Dr. Greenson's brother-in-law, Marilyn's lawyer, "Mickey" Rudin. One of Dr. Greenson's patients was Frank Sinatra, Marilyn's longtime flame. Dr. Engelberg, Marilyn's internist, was Dr. Greenson's friend.

When Marilyn decided to settle in Brentwood, Dr. Greenson recommended she hire Mrs. Murray, a longtime friend, something Marilyn did not know until later. Dr. Greenson had purchased his house from Mrs. Murray in the late Forties, and ironically, the house Marilyn bought on Helena Drive resembled Dr. Greenson's. The housekeeper brought with her into Marilyn's home her son-in-law, the handyman, Norman Jeffries II. Except for Pat Newcomb, the "handler" from Arthur Jacobs, the "Greenson Circle" around Marilyn was complete.

Mrs. Murray did not live at Marilyn's residence but would spend the night when Dr. Greenson thought his patient's condition required it. On August 4, the psychiatrist requested that she stay over. Pat Newcomb was there until late afternoon. At this point, Dr.

Greenson was in command. He asked Pat Newcomb to leave, as he believed she was upsetting Marilyn. When at about six o'clock Marilyn's masseur called, he told him, "She's out." He spent some time afterward talking to Marilyn in her bedroom, occasionally emerging to pace the hall in deep thought, according to Mrs. Murray, who observed him silently. Then he went home. At about seven o'clock, Joe DiMaggio Jr., with whom Marilyn had remained close, called and she talked to him. After that, she shut her bedroom door and went to sleep. Usually, when retiring for the night, she put the two telephones in a side room so she wouldn't be disturbed, but Dr. Greenson would inform police he found her clutching the telephone. This is one of the inconsistencies that has never been fully clarified. Who was Marilyn trying to reach when she died?

The criticism Mrs. Murray has come in for over the years mainly concerns her memory of time. She told Sgt. Clemmons the discovery of Marilyn's body took place about 12 midnight, and that the doctors arrived at approximately 12:30 A.M., in response to her telephone call for assistance. The police report has her discovering that something was wrong at around 3:35 in the morning, whereupon she called the doctors. The D.A. report concluded that "either Mrs. Murray misspoke in her statements to Clemmons, or Clemmons is in error, or Mrs. Murray was confused." As to Sgt. Clemmons's other observation that Mrs. Murray was displaying "abnormal behavior" by using the washing machine, cleaning out the refrigerator, and toting boxes to the car outside, the D.A. noted that "in stressful situations, persons often behave in bizarre ways."

Jack Clemmons told his superiors that he suspected

Marilyn Monroe might have been murdered. The D.A. then checked police files to see whether or not Clemmons had the qualifications to make this determination. It noted that he had worked for the Department from 1950 to 1965 and that within this period his total investigative experience amounted to about one year. But the investigator is not a recording machine. He does not merely see, but also senses, and the "smirk" on Dr. Greenson's face, the "remorseful" Engelberg, the "scared" housekeeper, the body serenely stretched across the bed which appeared to have been artificially placed, "swanlike"—these are part of the sense which apprehends the truth of an impression, and which made Sgt. Clemmons an intelligent observer. Investigative experience is extremely valuable, but it's not all that counts; I've actually found that a lack of experience may sometimes be helpful by seeing things with a fresh eye, not yet dulled by routine.

The policeman stated to the D.A. that the death scene did not appear to be "kosher." He did not think Mrs. Murray was "confused." Piqued with her domestic fuss, he was told by the housekeeper that she was "tidying up" because the Coroner was going to "seal up" the house. Normally, Clemmons later told reporters, it was extraordinary for someone to have this foresight at a time when there's usually more grieving than concern over perishables in the refrigerator and transferring little baskets and boxes to the car.

Although the D.A. dismissed the observations of the police sergeant as having "little evidentiary significance," he could not easily ignore my client's findings when purporting to examine the chief mystery of Marilyn's last day—the visit of Robert Kennedy to her house in the late afternoon. The D.A. report states that Slatzer "interviewed a Miss Elizabeth Pollard who related to him that Robert Kennedy and an unidentified male, believed to be a physician, were seen at the Monroe residence on August 4, 1962."

The neighbor in question recalled having been told by her late mother of a card party that Saturday afternoon, when looking up from her hand her mother suddenly exclaimed, "Look, girls, there he is *again!*" All the ladies were fairly elderly, but they threw down their cards and bustled to the window to see Bobby Kennedy entering Marilyn Monroe's residence with an unidentified man who was carrying what looked like a "medical bag."

The D.A.'s men took great pains to prove that the card-playing ladies could not possibly have seen Robert Kennedy without a great deal of contortion and lucky timing. Visiting the Monroe residence two decades after Marilyn's death, the probers took photographs of surrounding residences and the places from which Marilyn's house could be observed. The investigators noted that since Marilyn's house was at the left end of an alleylike cul-de-sac, it offered no direct view of the front of the property, so that the casual observation of persons arriving at her gate "could occur only if the occupant of a neighboring residence looked out a window facing the alley at the exact moment those persons traveled past that limited vantage point."

In order to see for myself what the D.A. meant, I took a walk in Marilyn's neighborhood one day in August at 5:00 P.M., the approximate time the card-playing ladies interrupted their game to see the brother of the President. If I were a prominent figure visiting a notorious sex symbol, I'd have a very good reason for not wanting to create a disturbance by driving to the end of a small cul-de-sac, so I put myself in step with an imaginary companion carrying a "medical bag" and walked down the short block on Fifth Helena Drive, that is, from the main street running off Sunset Boulevard, Carmelina Drive, to Marilyn's house. I could see the house where on that August day the ladies grouped by the window to titter at the famous person on the street below.

The house is much closer to Carmelina Drive than to the entrance of Marilyn's former residence. I was able to establish that from the upstairs card room one could look out and see who was going down Fifth Helena Drive. Marilyn's gates and front entrance were, indeed, highly visible.

The problem was not the "vantage point" of the card-playing ladies, however. Mrs. Murray said she was home all that day Saturday and would have seen Robert Kennedy if he had visited Marilyn. The D.A. report noted that during the original police investigation Joe DiMaggio Jr. said that on August 4 he had telephoned Marilyn at 2:00 P.M., 4:30 P.M., and 7:00 P.M. and that in each instance his call was answered by Mrs. Murray, which apparently bore out the housekeeper's statements. There are, however, two-and-a-half hour gaps between the calls, and a particularly crucial one between 4:30 P.M. and 7:00 P.M.

Surprisingly, Mrs. Murray did not deny this when my client spoke with her in 1973. In a taped interview, she affirmed that she indeed went out for a "couple of hours or more" that afternoon, allegedly to go to her apartment and get some things in order to spend the night. After the "light under the door," this was her second major retraction. A third was still to come, many years later, more astonishing yet. She was then almost eighty years old, and perhaps no longer "scared."

The D.A. report disappointed because it never went beyond the level of the "threshold examination." Nevertheless, it represented a real victory for my client, and more modestly, a victory for me. On all critical points, it rewarded my faith in him. He had come to me one day with Al Stump and made a compelling case for the possibility of foul play in Marilyn's death; he had detailed to my unbelieving ears the Kennedy role in Marilyn's final months; he had told me how the cover-up worked—and my own independent investigation turned up evidence that my client was sound across the board. Slatzer had had the Marilyn Conspiracy in its essential form, but many of his allegations still needed proof. The 1975 Church hearings gave authenticity to Marilyn's diary entries, and the 1982 D.A. report surprisingly performed a similar service by verifying my client on the vital element of the cover-up: Bobby's relations with Marilyn Monroe.

It affirmed this in an interview conducted by investigators with the aging housekeeper. Mrs. Murray's answers gave incontrovertible proof of my client's longstanding belief that she was less than candid to the original police investigators—in fact, this police report itself characterized her as "vague and evasive." Slatzer was very much aware Mrs. Murray knew Marilyn received Bobby. After all, he had had it from Marilyn herself; and his suspicions were shown to have been warranted when the 1982 D.A. report made the sensational admission, never before officially stated, that the Attorney General had visited Marilyn on at least one occasion, and that the housekeeper had been present; Bobby, according to the report, had arrived in the neighborhood in an open Cadillac convertible to pay a "social call to Miss Monroe thanking her for singing at John F. Kennedy's birthday celebration weeks earlier." That put it around June, about the time Marilyn first confided to my client that Robert Kennedy had promised to marry her. The report added, "This highly visible visit to the Monroe residence is corroborated by the housekeeper, who recalls such a visit."

For the first time—officially—Bobby was connected to visiting Marilyn. The D.A. alluded to this information in his report as "factual discrepancies and unanswered questions." Among these was the astonishing find made by the D.A.'s investigators of Marilyn's missing telephone records. Back in 1962, the logs had vanished from telephone company files and to those like Slatzer, already suspecting the curious circumstances surrounding Marilyn's death, nothing showed more flagrantly the cover-up than the mysterious removal of this vital evidence.

What could have revealed more clearly that the facts of the case were being suppressed? My client had long fought over this issue with the L.A. Police Department. He had even had an eyeball-to-eyeball showdown with Police Chief Parker. Slatzer had been tipped off and he knew where the records were. There were many parts to the cover-up. It involved many people and agencies at different points: a clerk who files away the Miner Memorandum, a housekeeper who is "confused," a Coroner who performs an autopsy that's "incomplete," and a police chief who for many years conceals the records listing the calls Marilyn made in the last weeks of her life. After twenty years, the D.A. report vindicated my client by turning up Marilyn's logs in the place where all along Bob knew they'd be found.

All these revelations should have prompted the L.A. County District Attorney's office to turn over its information to the Grand Jury. Before the Grand Jury, people must testify under oath. Many of the witnesses to what happened the night Marilyn died could no longer be called because they were dead. But apart from Mrs. Murray, two people were still alive in 1982 who had also seen or spoken to Marilyn on that fateful Saturday evening. Among the last to see Marilyn alive was Pat Newcomb. Among the last to speak to her, according to his own account, was Peter Lawford.

After Marilyn Monroe was found dead, it seemed as if all three had synchronized their comments to the press concerning Marilyn's condition on the day she died. Their accounts were similar to that Dr. Greenson gave to Deputy District Attorney Miner. "She was in a very good mood, a very happy mood," Pat Newcomb was to tell reporters. Mrs. Murray, too, said there was nothing unusual, "Marilyn was in good spirits." Peter Lawford said he first called at seven o'clock to invite Marilyn to his house for dinner, and reported, "She said she felt happy and was going to bed." Three days after Marilyn's death, when police officers attempted to contact Lawford, they were informed by his secretary that the actor had taken an airplane to an unknown destination.

Pat Newcomb's name has always been in our "RTS" file, and in 1982 the D.A. investigators found her as "reluctant to speak" as she had been twenty years earlier. In her interview with Slatzer, Mrs. Murray complained that the public relations girl was in the habit of "brushing her aside," and, in reports given out to the press, they generally held opposing views. This was relatively unimportant on some points, such as whether Dr. Greenson had sent Pat away at about 6:30 P.M., as Mrs. Murray claimed, or whether she left of her own will, as Pat Newcomb maintained. On other points, it was essential. It became a crucial question to know whether Marilyn had eaten that day, in order to substantiate the Coroner's report that he had found Marilyn's stomach empty. Mrs. Murray told my client that Marilyn had had nothing to eat or drink that day. Pat Newcomb, on the contrary, told him that Mrs. Murray had fixed sandwiches for both Marilyn and her, which they had eaten. In fact, Pat Newcomb recalled that they had eaten a "herb omelette," the housekeeper's specialty.

The principals who shared Marilyn's final hours have ever been elusive and "RTS." Nearly a quarter century after Marilyn's death, the contradictory statements of those who shared her last hours are impossible to sort out. They've involved one another in a slew of contradictions, and have contradicted themselves. In 1982, Peter Lawford recalled for the D.A. inspectors that he had received word that Marilyn was dead at 1:30 A.M. Mrs. Murray, after first telling Clemmons she had found the body at 12:30 A.M., told police she did not discover anything was wrong until 3:35 A.M. Pat Newcomb said she had learned Marilyn was dead at 4:00 A.M., before the police were called, from "Mickey" Rudin who had telephoned her from Marilyn's residence. And so it goes for all their statements except for one, on which all were agreed, some until their own deaths, others still to this day. On this item they remained consistent; from this point none departed. On the weekend Marilyn died, Pat Newcomb believed Robert Kennedy was on the "East Coast."

For a long time, Mrs. Murray didn't seem to know who Bobby Kennedy was, let alone where. Lawford was adamant that on August 4th or 5th Bobby Kennedy was not in the Los Angeles area, nor in California.

When asked about an affair between Bobby and Marilyn, Lawford said, "The whole thing about an affair is balls."

Chapter Seven

THE CORONER

Dr. Noguchi admitted that his autopsy had been "incomplete" . . . he said that he could not be positive Marilyn was not murdered with an injection of the barbituate that killed her.

Finally, I had the chance to talk to Dr. Hyman Engelberg, the only person on the scene of Marilyn's death who has never spoken out in public. Back in 1962, Dr. Curphey's Suicide Investigation Team talked to him, but it's not known what he said. Dr. Greenson, Mrs. Murray, Pat Newcomb, even though speaking in riddles, did occasionally talk. Dr. Engelberg never made a "comment." I knew that in the early hours of August 5 he had pronounced Marilyn Monroe dead by suicide. I also knew that there remains to this day a mystery about his prescription. Did he prescribe fifty Nembutal pills for Marilyn, as he claimed, or, as the L.A. Police Department reported, twenty-five? I was looking forward to our meeting. There were a lot of questions I wanted to ask him.

The difference in Engelberg's Nembutal count is

crucial. The 1982 D.A. report tried to grapple with this "factual discrepancy."

"Our investigators attempted to reconstruct the number of Nembutal capsules ingested by Miss Monroe, based on her blood and liver levels of the drugs," the report said, continuing, "Pathologists with whom our investigators consulted . . . estimated that she would have taken in excess of twenty-five pills, possibly as many as forty or more."

In the original police reports, Dr. Engelberg is recorded as stating that he prescribed fifty pills for Marilyn Monroe on the day before she died. At the scene of her death, fifteen bottles were found, eight of which were supplied to the Coroner's office. The seven vials not listed apparently were nonprescription, according to the mortician Guy Hockett. Included in the inventory were several vials of Librium, one each of Sulfathalidine, Noludar, Phenergan, and some pink capsules in a container without a label. One container was labeled Chloral Hydrate #50, prescribed on July 25, 1962; there was an empty container, prescribed by Dr. Engelberg, labeled, "#20858, 8-3-62, Nembutal, 1½ gr. #25." The D.A. report noted: "The statements attributed to Dr. Engelberg concerning the prescription or refill for 50 pills are inconsistent with the physical evidence indicating only 25 pills were prescribed by him on August 3, 1962." Neither were the "twenty-five pills" in agreement with the toxicology report from the Coroner's office, indicating that as many as 47 would have been required to supply the dosages found in her liver and blood samples.

Marilyn died of a heavy concentration of barbiturates in her blood, enough to kill any healthy person. Where did she get the pills to make up the fatal dosage?

The question has never been answered. Was the excess dosage administered through a "hot shot," a "rapid-acting instrumentality," such as hypodermic injection? Or through the application of "proctoclysis," an enema, using a syringe? In the D.A. investigation, the man in charge, Deputy District Attorney Mike Carroll, said, "There were two areas that caused us some concern. One was the source of medication."

This was one of the questions I wanted to ask the doctor. Another question concerned the curious admission made by Dr. Greenson to the journalist Maurice Zolotow that he had arrived on the death scene before Dr. Engelberg, and "did not see the Nembutal bottle on her night table." According to the doctors I consulted for this investigation, Marilyn Monroe appeared to have obtained lethal amounts of Nembutal and toxic, if not lethal, amounts of Chloral Hydrate in the ordinary course of treatment by her local physicians. In that connection, I had a question of general philosophical interest in the area of pharmaceutical and medical responsibility in prescription drug overdose cases. When at last Engelberg and I met, typical for Los Angeles, our encounter took place on television.

It happened about two months after my news conference. I was at the office when I picked up a call on my personal box and heard the voice of Alicia Sandoval. She hosted a popular live afternoon show, "Open Line," on Station KTTV. "My guest today is going to be Dr. Hyman Engelberg, who pronounced Marilyn Monroe dead." She asked, "Would you like to question him on television?"

"How tough can my question be?" I immediately responded. "And how long will I have?"

I could ask anything I liked, she said; I could stay on

128

the air as long as the session kept going, but since she did not want to start the program with Dr. Engelberg walking off angrily, the station would hold my call for at least five minutes after his appearance began. There was an hour till broadcast time, and I was given a special hotline number to call. Dr. Engelberg was scheduled to discuss heart attacks, plugging a recent book he'd written on his experience in the cardiac field.

I'd been on "Open Line" earlier as call-in guest in a discussion on missing persons, and again sometime afterward I was "in-studio" to discuss my investigation into Marilyn Monroe's death on the occasion of the twentieth anniversary. This time I sat down at my desk to jot down six or seven questions. Professional investigators know that the most difficult part of their job is to get the subject talking. That's why during interrogations they make the first question easy to answer. My first question was a little "push," designed to get Engelberg off the mark.

I turned on my office television to Channel 11 so I could watch the show while talking. I had the hotline number written on a pad in front of me. Some of the secretarial staff and agents joined me in my office. Everyone had a special interest in our longest-running case. Privately, I didn't expect much to come of the discussion. Someone who had been silent for as long as Engelberg was not going to break it before the television camera, I thought.

The first caller discussed heart attacks. Dr. Engelberg, quoting from his book, sounded fluent, even melodious. He had the calm voice of a person used to dealing with anxious, excitable people. We welcome that voice in times of crisis because it gives strength, but in normal health we find it tedious; I waited impatiently for him to finish answering the question. The minutes crept by. I would be the next caller. Being an "observer" by profession, I believe that we show what we feel, even though a detective may have to look for it in signs undetectable to the layman. The Deputy D.A. and his men were pros, and I had advised them to watch the program; I particularly wanted them to see Engelberg's "reaction."

The person screening the calls put me through, and once on the air, unlike regular callers who give only first names, I fully identified myself, adding, "I'm the investigator who has worked on the Marilyn Monroe case for over ten years."

I wanted to ask a "lead question," one that would open the subject of bruises found on Marilyn's body. Dr. Noguchi's autopsy report stated that "no needle marks were found." However, both Doctors Engelberg and Greenson submitted claims to probate, to be paid by Marilyn's estate. Dr. Engelberg's claim was for an injection he gave Marilyn on August 3, including a visit to her home. Dr. Greenson stated he saw Marilyn seven times from July 30, 1962, through August 4, when he saw her at her home; all other visits, including two on August 2, were in his office. Dr. Engelberg stated the dates of injections prior to her death; Dr. Greenson did not, yet psychiatrists, as we know, do give their patients injections. I wanted to touch upon these different points and ask Engelberg, as the doctor who pronounced Marilyn dead, whether he'd noticed the widely reported bruises.

"Possibly," I said, "you could clear up a couple of questions. On August 3, the day before Marilyn died, you gave her an injection according to the probate claim you submitted, and I wonder if you could tell what the injection was for. Why wasn't it shown on the autopsy? Is it not normal for an injection to leave a mark for some time?"

I watched his "reaction" on television. Dr. Engelberg stared in the air. He said he did not hear the question. It was repeated. There was a long pause. He replied, "I'm not interested in talking about Marilyn Monroe on this program. I won't answer any questions about her at this time."

On my television screen, a normally composed figure with a melodious voice had "reacted" in an agitated manner. Off-camera during a commercial break, Alicia told me afterward, Engelberg had been "very, very nervous."

About a month later, watching the local ABC-TV News, I found myself listening with a great deal of interest as the same subject was again being aired. But this time the speaker was far from reticent. Dr. Noguchi was saying some astonishing things. More than twenty years after performing the autopsy on his most famous case, he admitted on television that there were bruises on Marilyn Monroe's back and hip that have never been explained. He was actually calling for a new inquiry into her death. I thought it remarkable that Marilyn Monroe's body was finally to have the inquest it should have had twenty years ago. "Those involved should be willing to entertain new information," Noguchi said, two decades after signing the original Coroner's report, where he had penciled in "probable" next to "suicide," as Marilyn's cause of death.

According to a source in the Coroner's office, Marilyn's original body diagrams, both anterior and posterior, showed bruises in the places Dr. Noguchi mentioned. On the chart that was available in 1962 only one bruise remained. My client, seeking an opinion removed from a possible prejudiced L.A. County, where Dr. Noguchi had become a political issue, conferred with a distinguished forensic pathologist, Dr. Sidney Weinberg, Chief Medical Examiner of Suffolk County in New York. The bruise visible on the 1962 chart was on the upper part of Marilyn's left hip; Dr. Weinberg stated that it looked very much "like an injection site." On the TV news show, looking straight ahead, as if he were directly addressing Dr. Weinberg in faraway New York, Dr. Noguchi admitted that the bruise was a mystery that had bothered him for years. When asked if her death could have been murder, he said, "It could have."

The next day, in a follow-up interview in the *Herald Examiner,* Dr. Noguchi said that in 1962 authorities could have ruled out murder if the contents of Marilyn's stomach and intestines had been analyzed. These organs would have contained traces of the chemicals if the victim had swallowed the sleeping pills. As it was, no traces were found in the stomach and intestines. If such drugs are injected, he said, they leave traces only in the liver and blood, where his autopsy did reveal the evidence of "barbiturate overdose." But because investigators found an empty pill bottle by her bed, Noguchi explained, they decided that the actress had swallowed the pills, killing herself, and automatically ruled out foul play—*before* conducting the actual lab tests to determine the cause of death.

With this astounding reversal of himself for the first time in two decades, Dr. Noguchi admitted that his autopsy had been "incomplete." He acknowledged what my client and I had been years in bringing to light. He was coming round to seeing things the way his critics had been urging him to, by pointing out the inadequacy of his own autopsy report.

On the same television show, Dr. Noguchi said he was sorry the lab work was either never completed or was missing. By this, he presumably meant that if he'd known what really went on the night Marilyn died, he might have proceeded differently in his examination; he'd probably have insisted the lab work be completed or, if missing, that it be found. He'd have done the tests, which I believe would bear out my long-held conviction that Marilyn was murdered by injection.

It was strange, after the long years my client and I had worked to demonstrate the inadequacy of the autopsy report, to hear Dr. Noguchi declare himself in agreement with us. Nearly a quarter century after Marilyn's death, he said that he could not be positive Marilyn was not murdered with an injection of the barbiturate that killed her.

What killed Marilyn Monroe was Nembutal, a member of the barbiturate group under the category "Sedatives and Hypnotics," with the generic name "pentobarbital." According to the report of the Chemical Analysis signed by Chief Toxicologist, Dr. R. J. Abernathy, there was 13.0 mg. percent pentobarbital in the liver and 4.5 mg. percent in Marilyn's blood. Chloral Hydrate (phenobarbital), also known as "knockout drops," in liquid form was present in 8 mg. percent in her blood. The street name for Nembutal is "yellowjackets," because the drug has a yellow dye in the gel. This coloring agent leaves a stain in the digestive tract of the person taking the pills.

Nembutal comes in four forms: yellow capsules, colorless syrup, injectionable liquid, and suppository.

Marilyn was taking the 1½-grain yellow capsules, the strongest available in capsule form. According to the toxicologist, twenty-five "yellowjackets" would have been insufficient to raise the barbiturate level in the blood to 4.5 mg. percent and 13 mg. percent pentobarbital in the liver. Medical authorities I consulted in my study of Dr. Noguchi's autopsy state that 3.3 mg. percent of Nembutal is lethal, even to a heavy user of this sleeping compound. Yet when Dr. Noguchi did Marilyn's autopsy, no Nembutal was found in her digestive system, nor any trace of the yellow dye.

Based on his examination, Dr. Noguchi concluded that Marilyn Monroe died as a result of acute barbiturate poisoning, "due to an ingestion of overdose." What this means is that she took the pills by her mouth rather than having the fatal dosage of Nembutal introduced through any other channel, which may have included either suppository or needle, the so-called "hot shot." Thus, without a comprehensive series of tests to rule out these alternative modes of entry, the Coroner's office continued to accept the "suicide" version as reported by police investigators. Nearly twenty-five years later, the failure to do these tests led Dr. Noguchi to suggest that the statements made in the police report may have caused him to overlook the possibility of "foul play." Noguchi said last year to another investigator into Marilyn's death, "It seemed to me . . . that it's very likely the Police Department did close things down."

Given the admittedly limited findings of the Coroner's office, I focused my investigation on the premise that Marilyn had taken the dosage orally as outlined in the Coroner's report. However, this scenario proved to be impossible for two reasons. Had she taken all of these capsules orally, the coroner should have found two things: yellow dye stains in the tissues of the digestive tract from the esophagus all the way down to the small and large intestines; and the residue of 47–50 "yellowjackets" either partially dissolved or completely undissolved. Dr. Noguchi found no yellow stain, much less any trace of the Nembutal capsules. What he found in Marilyn's stomach was about 20 cc. (equivalent to a teaspoonful) of what he referred to as "brown mucoid fluid." This was sent for lab work to Dr. Abernathy.

The toxicologist boiled down the fluid in a beaker to crytals which he examined under a polarized microscope. As each drug has an individual structure, much like a snowflake, the toxicologist can recognize Seconal, Chloral Hydrate, Nembutal, or any barbiturate by its molecular configuration. The toxicologist noted no residue of pills in the gastric contents. There was no sign of the barbiturates in the kidneys. Dr. Noguchi examined the contents of the duodenum under the polarized microscope and here, too, discovered no refractile crystals, "meaning," he wrote, "it was found to be empty."

Here the bickering between Pat Newcomb and Mrs. Murray throws an interesting sidelight on the Coroner issue. Mrs. Murray told Bob Slatzer that on the afternoon of August 4 she fixed Pat Newcomb an herb omelette made from herbs picked from the little garden Marilyn kept in a special plot between the garage and the guest house. Marilyn, she said, did not eat anything but only drank some fruit juice. Pat Newcomb, however, recalled to Slatzer that she and Marilyn had eaten hamburgers that afternoon. In this instance, I am inclined to favor the housekeeper, since Pat Newcomb told police investigators that on the evening of August 3, the evening before her death—the evening when Slatzer had spoken with Marilyn from Columbus, Ohio, and found her distraught and threatening to hold the news conference—Pat remembered having been with a cheerful Marilyn at a restaurant. However, Newcomb could not remember the name of the restaurant, nor where it was located, nor what she had for dinner. If Mrs. Murray was correct and Marilyn had eaten, her stomach would not be "empty." In that event, what happened to the food?

But I'm satisfied to leave the question of whether or not Marilyn ate a hamburger or Pat Newcomb an herb omelette one of the minor mysteries in the case. It is not vital to the conclusions that can be drawn from the Coroner's report, which bear out the results of my investigative findings. Based on Dr. Noguchi's autopsy report, I do not think Marilyn killed herself by swallowing a lethal dosage of Nembutal. If Marilyn had swallowed the pills, they would first have been broken down in the stomach and then absorbed through the duodenum, which connects the stomach to the small intestine. From the duodenum, the partially dissolved or undissolved barbiturates would have been carried in the blood to the liver, then from the liver back again into the blood to the kidneys as waste matter to be excreted. The toxicology lab found no signs of barbiturates in the kidneys, just as it found none in the stomach and duodenum. The high amount of barbiturates in Marilyn's body was concentrated in the blood and liver. This meant that the amount of drugs found in her system could not have been ingested by swallowing alone. And so Dr. Noguchi's own autopsy results led me to oppose his statement that Marilyn died through an "oral ingestion of overdose." The stomach and duodenum had been bypassed in the physical absorption process of the Nembutal, and the only way to bypass the digestive organs would be by introduction of the drug directly into the blood.

I consulted a number of experts with impeccable credentials and found them in agreement with each other in supporting my own conclusions. Dr. Weinberg, the noted New York forensic pathologist, after studying the autopsy report, stated that its findings were "certainly not characteristic of an oral ingestion of large amounts of barbiturates. One must seriously consider the possibility of an injection or the use of a suppository to account for the toxicology findings." The equally distinguished E. Forrest Chapman of Belleville, Michigan, concluded from his study of Dr. Noguchi's findings that they "furnish high suspicion. The total absence in the digestive tract of a barbiturate, even microscopic crystals of same, indicates a non-oral route of administration. And in the absence of a needle and syringe on the premises, the above conclusions are partially or fully warranted."

The medical authorities I consulted provided me with a firsthand education in the functioning of the internal human anatomy. They told me it is practically unheard-of for a person who has swallowed a lethal dose of "sleep-inducers" not to have refractile crystals in the digestive system. I also sought out their advice, as well as that of the manufacturer of Nembutal, about the yellow dye which stains the tissues of the digestive tract. This longstanding controversy in the Marilyn case was taken up as well by the 1982 D.A. report. The D.A.'s investigators noted that "empirical information is contrary to the yellow dye trail supposition." But the spokesman for Abbott Laboratories, the maker of Nembutal, whom I contacted, confirmed that the drug's yellow dye normally leaves a stain in the mucous tissues. I received the same answer from experts referred to me by the American Medical Association in New York. One told me that when a suspected victim of a Nembutal overdose is brought to him for examination, the first thing he looks for is the yellow dye. If the tissues are red, the drug in question is usually Seconal, a sleeping capsule with a red dye in the gel.

Some sign of the yellow dye should have been present if Marilyn had ingested the Nembutal by swallowing the pills in such large quantities and within the short time indicated by Noguchi's superior, L.A. County Coroner Dr. Theodore Curphey, who was then in charge of the Marilyn investigation. The absence of Nembutal dye would occur if the drug had been introduced through a non-oral form by injection or suppository. The only other explanation for the lack of yellow dye found by Noguchi in Marilyn's digestive system would be that she swallowed the capsules over a long period of time on the fateful day of August 4; in that case, the yellow dye would have had a chance to dissipate. But according to Dr. Curphey, speaking at his 1962 press conference, Marilyn had swallowed the capsules "in one gulp within a period of seconds."

At the time of Dr. Noguchi's original findings, the Coroner's office joined the theme struck by Marilyn's two doctors at the death scene and the Police Department in claiming that Marilyn died by her own hand. The scientific justification seemed to lie in the findings of the Toxicology report, which bore out that Marilyn had swallowed the pills rather than having received her fatal dosage by any other means, such as by suppository or "hot shot." In 1985, I had the opportunity for the first time to obtain the toxicology report from File No. 81128, the case report of the death of Marilyn Monroe. This had not been made public before. In fact, until this report was released, not even Dr. Noguchi could remember all the details. He couldn't remember, by his own admission, anyone present at the time the autopsy was conducted. It was only by accident that the Miner Memorandum revealed that John Miner, the Legal-Medical Head at the D.A.'s office, was an eyewitness at the actual autopsy.

Tracing Dr. Noguchi's steps twenty-three years ago, I learned from these newly released documents that the Toxicology laboratory supplied only one part of the picture. At Dr. Noguchi's request, it did a routine "Report of Chemical Analysis," limiting the examination to the pentobarbital and Chloral Hydrate contained in the vials found at Marilyn's bedside. The findings of 13.0 mg. percent pentobarbital in the liver, and 4.5 mg. percent in the blood satisfied the determination of suicide that had already been made in the minds of the investigators before any tests had been done.

The reason this ratio is considered significant is that the two figures seemed to match up with the process that occurs when someone swallows a toxic level of medication. The Coroner's office and the Toxicologist drew their conclusions from the manner in which toxic substances when swallowed pass through a victim's body. Taken orally, they follow a pathway through the body's system, leaving a trail of their origins—traces in the mouth, esophagus, stomach, intestines, blood and liver, in that order. Although Marilyn's blood/liver pentobarbital ratio might have occurred via the oral ingestion of a massive dosage, the empty stomach and lack of yellow gel point to a different mode of drug entry. Pentobarbital by injection is the likeliest cause for the relationship of the percentages of the drug found in the blood and in the liver; injected, they leave only traces in the liver and blood, and in order to rule out that Marilyn Monroe had died by a "hot shot," the L.A. County Coroner should have ordered Marilyn's intestines to be examined, since as part of the pathway through which drugs travel to the blood and liver they should have left a residue there as well. In 1982, the District Attorney's report stated that more sensitive tests on the stomach lining and contents were not performed by Noguchi. "It is Dr. Noguchi's position," the report notes, "that in the absence of circumstances pointing to facts contrary to what he observed during the autopsy (i.e., some sinister overtones to the death), the more sensitive chemical analyses were, under the guidelines then in existence in the Coroner's office, not properly performed."

The media jumped on his statement, allowing Noguchi to be "newsmaker" for a few days. But these same enterprising reporters might have had the story some ten years earlier if they'd properly pursued the line of dogged investigative work suggested by a most revealing statement from the pathologist who was then L.A. County Coroner.

In a 1973 interview with Norman Mailer for a book he was doing on Marilyn Monroe, the Coroner admitted for the first time that a sample of Marilyn's small intestine actually was taken, although not tested; by the time questions about Marilyn's possible murder surfaced two or three months after her death, Dr. Noguchi said the specimens had been routinely destroyed. According to the autopsy report, Dr. Noguchi

checked the stomach and duodenum, w̶ [...]
the stomach and small intestine, only und[...]
microscope for drug and pill particles. Bu[...]
experts I've consulted agree that the small i̶ [...]
would have been the storage place of any partially or
undissolved Nembutal capsules. At the very least,
given the condition of Marilyn's blood and liver, it
should have contained some evidence of microscopic
crystals, if not of the yellow dye. The significance of
the untested and discarded small intestine of Marilyn
Monroe was not noted except by a few people with a
special interest, such as Mailer, Slatzer, and myself.

Dr. Noguchi said that the sample of Marilyn's small
intestine was not tested because at the time there were
no facilities in the County Coroner's office for making
such tests. I found this difficult to believe and after
checking with some pathologists discovered that even
if the Coroner's office lacked the equipment, it was
readily available at hospitals and several university
medical centers nearby. In his autopsy report Dr.
Noguchi wrote, "The remainder of the small intestine
shows no gross abnormalities." I asked myself why, if
there were no "gross abnormalities," he had taken out
the specimen in the first place. And furthermore, if it
could not be tested, why was it taken out as a sample
along with other vital organs?

These were among the questions we posed in 1974 to
the Grand Jury of L.A. County requesting a reopening
of the Marilyn case. Our request was denied. Ten
members of the twenty-three member Grand Jury
which decides on such matters stated that there was no
necessity for reopening the matter. In our letter, antici-
pating their objection, we tried to show that the 1962
investigation was flawed by its own limitations. Every-

body involved, from the two doctors in the death bedroom to the Coroner, put the cart before the horse. They came to the conclusion of suicide based on impressions and hearsay rather than hard scientific evidence. At the very beginning of the case, Sgt. Clemmons, the first law enforcement officer on Marilyn's death scene, observed that the two doctors seemed eager to create the impression of suicide. According to the two police reports, Dr. Greenson and Dr. Engelberg stated in the death bedroom that since the Nembutal bottle was empty, Marilyn must have necessarily died of taking these "missing capsules." Sgt. Clemmons thought it was extremely prejudicial for such a decision to be made before the Coroner had completed his autopsy.

Sgt. Clemmons was the first to question a suicide verdict that seemed to be already official before the body was taken out of the house. The whole scene to him looked "arranged"—Marilyn Monroe "swan-like," as if the death-dealing dosage which, Clemmons's experience had shown, often contorted, jolted, convulsed and choked the victim, in Marilyn's death acted to fold the limbs in smoothness for her last nude shot. In Clemmons's description of the death scene, the bathroom showed an orderly arrangement of toiletries. In the bedroom, handwoven "cobra" baskets, a pile of neatly folded clothes, and a stack of purses stood against the walls. The pill bottles, except for the empty Nembutal bottle lying on its side, seemed methodically set up. To the bluff, straight-talking policeman it didn't look "kosher."

It was obvious that had someone been planning to murder Marilyn, he would make it appear a suicide through Marilyn's well-publicized involvement with certain "sleep-inducing" medications. It was also apparent that he would want to leave behind an orderly death scene. But as Sgt. Clemmons was the first to notice, the scrupulous killer had forgotten to place a glass on the nightstand. By this omission, he created another "factual discrepancy" that has never been explained by police investigators, Deputy D.A. Carroll's team located one published photograph that "appears" to show a drinking vessel. Their report states, "The absence of a drinking glass or other liquid container would not be dispositive [sic], however, because Miss Monroe could have taken the pills in her bathroom many minutes before she became unconscious in her bed." But Marilyn's bathroom on the night she died was out of order due to remodeling, and Mrs. Murray said she was never wakened to bring water. In his 1974 letter to the L.A. County Grand Jury, Bob Slatzer included among his evidence a reference to his as-yet-unexplained mystery: "No drinking glass was found in Marilyn Monroe's room, and having known the actress quite well for a sixteen-year period, I have personal knowledge that she could not consume capsules without some type of fluid such as milk or water."

Rather than having the police act on the suspicions of Sgt. Clemmons, the first "outsider" on the death scene, the authorities listened to Coroner Curphey who on Monday, August 6, based on the autopsy results, referred the case to the L.A. Suicide Prevention Center, which appointed a team to make the final determination of how Marilyn died. Dr. Curphey told the press that he was going all-out to get every bit of available information so that no stone would be left unturned in finding the cause of the actress's purported "suicide."

The team was composed of three mental health experts, Drs. Robert E. Litman, Norman Farberow, and Norman Tabachnich. Dr. Farberow outlined the scope of the team's work to newsmen. "We are interviewing anybody and everybody." Of those with the most valuable testimony regarding Marilyn's final hours, the team interviewed Pat Newcomb, Dr. Engelberg and Dr. Greenson, but not Mrs. Murray, nor did it interview the two men who might have had most to say on Marilyn's mysterious demise, Robert Kennedy and Peter Lawford. Bobby's brother-in-law would have been a logical candidate for elucidating the kind of information they were seeking, since the press had already printed that he had spoken to Marilyn by telephone shortly before her death. Neither Jack nor Robert Kennedy was questioned, even though one of the psychiatrists on the Suicide Team, Dr. Littman, supposed, as the result of his interviews with Dr. Greenson, that the Kennedys were involved in Marilyn's final days. Twenty-two years later, Littman admitted to another investigator that he did not believe Greenson had completely "leveled" with him in 1962 on some of the questions regarding Marilyn's death.

It was perhaps not at all unusual that Dr. Greenson became the most fruitful source for the Suicide Team's information. They were all psychiatrists; they all spoke the same professional jargon. From Marilyn's psychiatrist, Littman learned that his famous patient had become involved before her death with "very important men in government." In 1984, five years after Dr. Greenson had died, Littman said he presumed the "very important" men were the Kennedys. Littman said he also presumed when he interviewed

144

Greenson that the "despondency" the psychiatrist referred to in his patient's final days had something to do with Marilyn having been "jilted" by one of the "important men."

Indicative of the team's purpose and its limitations was the fact that, like Dr. Noguchi, the team members from the very start of their investigation agreed that they were reporting on a "suicide." There was never any suggestion that Marilyn's death might have been anything else. The cause of death was already established and their job was to find out *why* she had laid hands on herself, not *how* she might have died.

The Police Department was not pressing for any further probing, and the County Coroner's abrupt announcement of Marilyn's death as "probable suicide" before the autopsy was hardly done meant that, according to the Coroner's office, Marilyn's suicide had been determined to be an "accident." When Dr. Noguchi's results were in, Dr. Curphey might have known by the light of his own professional expertise that the autopsy report contained a highly suspicious incongruity—the lack of pill residue in the stomach along with the high blood/liver barbiturate level. Here he should have changed direction, thanked the Suicide Team for its services, and called for an inquest. None of the testimony the Suicide Team heard was taken under oath. Its members utilized as their chief sources the two men who originally concluded that Marilyn's death was a suicide. Dr. Greenson told Dr. Littman that Marilyn had "often expressed wishes to give up, to withdraw, and even to die," while telling John Miner that Marilyn had been "making progress" and was looking forward to the future. At a Coroner's inquest, such inconsistencies, if not satisfactorily explained, might result in perjury charges, while no legal consequences attended the statements of witnesses made to the Suicide Team.

The Suicide Team's work was prejudiced from the beginning by its relying on Dr. Greenson for its "psychological profile." Dr. Greenson was hardly an impartial witness to a situation where his medical credibility was at stake. The version he told Miner was at odds with what he told Littman. We will never know what was on the Greenson tapes, possibly the most pertinent evidence as to Marilyn's state of mind in her final days, because the psychiatrist swore Miner to secrecy. Before a Coroner's Inquest, Miner would have to reveal this information or be cited for contempt.

Whether "despondency" and "rejection" were the cause of Marilyn's death, or merely an opportunity for those who plotted against her and saw in her emotional imbalance the chance to murder her, was unresolved by the Suicide Team report. It simply failed to conduct a thorough probe because of its heavy psychological emphasis. By limiting the inquiry to establish the "why" of the "suicide," the team omitted large areas of evidentiary value, including not only Lawford's role and the Kennedy connection, but also Marilyn's connections with Organized Crime. A very important item they might have investigated, as having possible links to her death, was Marilyn's visit in the company of Peter and Pat Lawford to Frank Sinatra at the Cal-Neva Lodge, which Sinatra reportedly owned jointly with Giancana. According to Peter Lawford, the only eyewitness to report on Marilyn's mysterious last visit to this lugubrious resort just a week before she died, the trip was a disaster. He stated to police that Marilyn had tried suicide. The visit was by other accounts a wretched stay that had her drunk, disoriented and disheveled, wandering through the lodge. She was

reportedly often unaware of her surroundings, including the presence of Frank Sinatra, who was then
headlining at the lodge. When half-sober, she called
friends to talk about the things going on around her, of
being pressured by Lawford into "orgies" and other
activities she did not want to get involved in.

What went on at Cal-Neva in the last week of her life
that caused her rapid disintegration? What connection
did this visit bear to her final slide to death? What was
conveyed to her, either by threats or innuendo, by the
men of Cal-Neva who inhabited both the underworld
and the world of the Kennedys? What happened at the
lodge that might have firmed her resolve to seek
revenge for her humiliation at this once-mob-infested
resort? Did it make her determined to fly in the face of
everyone, even herself, and plan to hold a sensational
press conference?

The Suicide Team never addressed itself to these
questions, which a brief study of Marilyn's final days
should have indicated as being significant. The report
it issued conveyed impressions largely given by Dr.
Greenson as to Marilyn's psychological condition.
These impressions were in direct contradiction to the
report which became the basis for the once-secret
Miner Memorandum. In the statement releasing the
findings of the Suicide Team two weeks after Marilyn's
death, County Coroner Theodore Curphey cited as
physical evidence the empty Nembutal bottle by her
bedside and the high level of barbiturates and chloral
hydrate in the blood. Curphey put even greater emphasis on Marilyn's history of "psychiatric disturbance."
He mentioned Marilyn Monroe's "severe fears and
frequent depressions," without going into the crucial
autopsy evidence of the empty stomach, which opened
the possibility of the death-dealing "hot shot," or

other "lethal instrumentality," such as a suppository. When at his news conference a reporter among the clamoring press corps shouted out to the County Coroner, "Who supplied the basis for your findings?", Dr. Curphey stated with great firmness, "We will not expose the names of the people who gave their accounts and reports to us in confidence."

Chief Coroner Curphey, by ignoring the possibility of any wrongdoing in Marilyn's death, choked off all official inquiries into the case for twenty years. The Board of Supervisors appoints the Coroner and it could have compelled him to reinvestigate the matter, but with an amazing alacrity, as if somehow there was relief that the sex goddess had fallen, everyone readily accepted County Coroner Curphey's statement of "probable suicide," on the basis of the information supplied by the Suicide Team. Dr. Littman's admission that he did not believe Dr. Greenson had been "totally candid" with him came twenty years after the case was officially closed.

It is in the light of a foregone verdict of suicide pronounced by the two doctors on the death scene that we must see Dr. Noguchi's autopsy results, as well as the fate of the Miner Memorandum, and the weakness of the conclusions drawn by the Suicide Team. Through the years, I've held the conviction that many people involved in the aftermath of Marilyn's death have always had doubts. That belief was strengthened when I heard some begin to voice their reservations following the fresh interest in the Marilyn case as the result of my widely publicized 1982 news conference. Of those who've recently spoken out and supported my demand for a new investigation, Dr. Noguchi has made the greatest impact by calling into question many aspects of the "suicide version," including his own autopsy results. I've always felt that if his report was "incomplete," it was not due to his negligence. He examined Marilyn Monroe on the basis of the "suicide" reports furnished by the mortuary attendant and police. Certain tests he'd certainly have done were homicide suspected were therefore omitted.

More important, perhaps, County Coroner Curphey had already made public that Marilyn's death was "probable suicide." As a young medical examiner, he could not very well, being a subordinate, go against his chief. Recently, he's voiced the wish that at the time he *had* insisted that all the organs be tested. He regrets that he didn't follow through with the analysis, especially of the intestines. "As a junior member of the staff," Dr. Noguchi apologized, "I didn't feel I could challenge the department head on procedures." As far as the autopsy went, in terms of Curphey's almost instantaneous ruling of "probable suicide" as the cause of Marilyn's death, Dr. Noguchi performed creditably. The pathologists consulted by the 1982 D.A. investigators all praised Dr. Noguchi's work as being thoroughly professional.

Apparently, besides the tests that were not done, Dr. Noguchi was also concerned about certain marks on Marilyn's body. I thought of my mystery informant, "Tom," describing the sounds recorded on Spindel's "Kennedy-Monroe" tapes—"the sound of a slap followed by the sound of a body striking the ground"—as I read Dr. Noguchi quoted in an interview that two decades after Marilyn's death the question of the unexplained bruise on Marilyn Monroe's lower back still haunted him.

Like the haunting question of the bruise which was

THE MARILYN CONSPIRACY

never resolved because of his limited investigation, Dr. Noguchi was similarly unable to pinpoint the exact manner in which the fatal dosage was administered. Conscious of the high concentration of barbiturates the lab found in Marilyn's blood, Dr. Noguchi pored over Marilyn's body with a hand-held magnifying glass in search of recent needle marks. But again his search suffered from the limits imposed by the "probable suicide" verdict that had already fixed itself in the minds of the investigators, including his own. When interviewed during the 1982 District Attorney's probe, Noguchi reported to investigators that he had "searched the whole body for needle marks and paid particular attention to those areas most commonly associated with the illegal injection of drugs." Again, with the absence of any possibility of foul play, the results of the coroner's examination became a self-fulfilling prophecy. Since Dr. Curphey had already decided on Marilyn's cause of death, no one in the Coroner's office could be expected to become the one responsible for "rocking the boat."

The determination of whether or not the high barbiturate levels found in Marilyn's blood were introduced by injection is vitally important for two reasons. Since it was known that Dr. Engelberg was giving Marilyn injections, the high dosage in the blood might have come about through medical malfeasance on the part of the physician. The second reason, and to my mind the more telling one, is that it might determine as well the possibility of foul play. Based on years of medical consultations and reviews of the medical literature on the case, I believe that evidence existed at the time that should have led the Coroner to consider that the fatal dosage was not swallowed, but may have entered the body through injection or a suppository.

150

The most important clue for me was the absence of capsules in the stomach while there were high pento-barbital concentrations found in Marilyn's blood and liver. Had Marilyn swallowed the barbiturates in a sudden dose, a residue should have been left in the stomach. The absence of this evidence suggests an alternative method of introducing the drug. Some have suggested that Marilyn ingested the pills over a long period of time on the last day of her life. It should be remembered that Dr. Greenson noted that Marilyn appeared to be "drugged" during his two visits to her home on August 4. According to this scenario, the fatal dose might have been just one too many on top of the previously ingested pills.

The only way to determine which of these modes of entry was responsible for the fatal dose was by examining the physical evidence, especially the intestines, which would have shown evidence of the barbiturates. The disposal of the upper intestine, remarked on by Dr. Noguchi, precluded the examination of that organ for capsule residue. But through discussing the Marilyn case with one of my medical advisers, I discovered that another important piece of physical evidence had been destroyed, the lower intestine. There might have been a third route of entry besides swallowing and the "hot shot"—"colonically," in the form of an enema. Enemas were a popular Hollywood health fad in those days. They were thought to cleanse the system, help reduce weight and bring relief to constipation. Marilyn followed the fad because she suffered chronically from constipation.

This medical adviser suggested that since Marilyn was embalmed and placed in a tomb, evidence might still be found to disprove that Marilyn swallowed 47 Nembutal pills. He believes that in her preserved condition, even after twenty-three years, specimens might still be taken. Since there were no drugs in the upper digestive system, the other route of administration, whether by injection or enema, might be found if the specimens are reexamined. Along with my medical adviser, I believe that the actual cause of Marilyn's death based on the physical evidence is yet to be determined. If Marilyn's body is exhumed, the mystery may end. Her death was not a suicide.

After investigating the Marilyn Conspiracy for six years, I felt I had passed the point of speculation and had hard evidence that Marilyn Monroe might have been murdered by the underworld with the silent acquiescence of the government's intelligence branch. In that year, we acquired an important piece of the puzzle. Unexpectedly, a witness whom we had long given up for lost surfaced. The remarkable information supplied by our "lost witness" about conditions in the Coroner's office—its unbelievable internal affairs—helped us get a better fix on the confusion surrounding the circumstances of Marilyn's death. We learned that the office had had a ring that stole credit cards from dead bodies; that specimens had routinely disappeared; that insurance company representatives, hoping to minimize their obligations to the estates of the deceased, had hovered around the county morgue; that there had been many unauthorized "viewings" of bodies; and that property belonging to the dead had routinely vanished from the Coroner's office locker.

From our contacts within the bureaucracy, we had been able to gather what it must have been like inside the Coroner's Office in the period between Marilyn's death and burial. I could recall the lugubrious horrors that came out of the testimony some years back from witnesses before the Civil Service Commission who accused Dr. Noguchi of "smiling" when he saw a great many bodies stacked up in the hallways during busy days at the morgue. The Coroner's office had long been a place of great turmoil. The record of the Civil Service Commission—which had heard Dr. Noguchi's appeal in the early Seventies after his dismissal as County Coroner by the Board of Supervisors—proves the state of near chaos that had prevailed in this abode of the dead. This normal state of confusion apparently had reached a peak when Marilyn's body was brought to the crypt. Our "lost witness" corroborated accounts we had previously received of the events that shook the Coroner's office after the body of the dead sex queen had arrived on the premises.

Slatzer met this ghost from the past in the course of a media appearance in the fall of 1978. My client was a guest on Los Angeles radio station KPOL on the occasion of a nostalgic tribute to Marilyn Monroe. In the silence of the sound studio, it almost seemed as if Los Angeles stood still. The songs sung by the tragic sex siren were suspended for two hours in a fluty whisper over her native city. There were fragments of dialogue full of suggestive repartee from the famous movies. Slatzer responded feelingly to the questions asked by the newscaster about the actress, who was inseparable from the memories of the most vibrant years of his life.

After the show, the program's sound recording engineer approached Slatzer and asked if he might see a copy of his book, *The Curious Life and Death,* which Slatzer had been reading from on the air. He disappeared with it into a quiet corner and, after a few minutes, returned. Holding open the book before Slatzer's curious eyes, he pointed to the page which showed a copy of Marilyn Monroe's death certificate. The young man's finger moved down to the lower corner of the page, and there Slatzer saw the familiar signature of the deputy coroner's aide whom he had tried to contact after Marilyn's autopsy, but whom he had never been able to find.

At that point, a hunch dawned on Slatzer, and just as he was about to cry out the name, the young man extended his hand and said, "I am Lionel Grandison."

Lionel Grandison turned out to be a most remarkable find, because almost immediately after introducing himself, he made the astonishing admission that among the property brought into the Coroner's office, there was a "book that looked like a red diary." He'd actually looked at it before it had abruptly disappeared. Flipping through the pages, he said he had seen references to the Kennedys, the Mafia and Cuba. He then confessed that he'd signed Marilyn Monroe's death certificate against his better judgment. He just didn't feel right about it, considering the circumstances, he said. But Dr. Curphey, the Chief Coroner, gave him his orders, and Dr. Curphey had asked him to sign it.

The tales of Lionel Grandison added a small volume to the rich chronicles of the Marilyn case. They shed light on the bizarre antics of the L.A. County Morgue. Grandison gave us information about the Coroner's office that needed to be taken with great caution; much of it was troubling, but enough matched with what I'd previously learned to paint a picture faithful to the context of Marilyn's post-mortem hours. It was necessary for us to take Lionel Grandison seriously on some counts and less seriously on others, as he had himself been embroiled a few months after Marilyn's autopsy on charges of certain improprieties. Grandison left the Coroner's office under a cloud, and afterward settled on a career in radio and television broadcasting.

I'm aware of the need to weigh evidence from a tainted source. My way of dealing with this type of informant is best illustrated by a story one of my special agents likes to tell about a notorious burglar who's the only survivor of a plane crash. In such a case, the first question is not about his larcenous activities, but about what happened that caused the plane to crash. Such a source, which may be compromised in some ways, may yet be truthful about conditions that do not implicate him.

Even if some of Grandison's testimony remains open to question, his accounts of disorder and laxity within the Coroner's office at the time have been affirmed by other sources with knowledge of the situation, who agree that this alarming state of affairs reached its peak upon the death of Marilyn Monroe, when even greater pressures than normal set the office awry.

The disorder then was so great that there are no supportive documents to be found in the Coroner's files concerning property belonging to Marilyn Monroe. The medical specimens have long since disappeared along with the slides and photographs. The correspondence between the Coroner's office and the District Attorney was, after the regular interval of time, purged from the files. The 1982 District Attorney's investigation could not determine even the most elementary factual matters relating to the case, not even how the body actually got to the Coroner's office downtown. It was unable to find out from any existing records whether or not the body was removed by the

Westwood Village Mortuary, or whether the Coroner's office took possession of the body at the scene. All the D.A.'s probers were able to learn was that the body was received by the Coroner staff personnel at 9 A.M. on August 5, 1962.

Grandison confirmed that many people were admitted into the Coroner's storage vault to "view" Marilyn for no reason other than that they were curious to see the corpse of the world's most highly publicized body. Just how easy it was to get into the facility was recently revealed by well-known Hollywood photographer Leigh Weiner, who was able to penetrate the cold storage room and snap a number of photographs of the famous corpse in Crypt 33, including the much-publicized picture of Marilyn's single toe protruding from the storage place with a death label hanging from it. Weiner had been able to enter the Coroner's vault simply by bribing the attendant with a bottle of Scotch. Under these conditions, would it be surprising if Marilyn's property, including the red diary, did disappear from the premises?

I was not satisfied, as the District Attorney apparently had been in 1982, to dismiss Grandison because in his lowly function as deputy coroner's aide, limited to routine paper and liaison work, he had had no "discretionary responsibility." Anyone, even in an unexalted position, can observe. As for his allegations that it was not unusual for property to disappear from the Coroner's office, the District Attorney's report quoted Dr. Noguchi that no property belonging to Marilyn Monroe had been received by the office. In the same report, however, Dr. Noguchi is also quoted as not being able to remember who was present at the autopsy, even though John Miner was there throughout his performance.

In such matters, I'm inclined to give fullest attention to the claim of the party privy to the inner workings of a situation, rather than to people who, twenty years after the fact, with few or no supporting documents, are quick to discredit the source without properly attempting to distinguish false from true statements. For this reason, I did not reject out of hand Lionel Grandison's confession that he had been forced to sign Marilyn Monroe's death certificate while entertaining grave misgivings about the propriety of the act. When Slatzer asked him why, if he had had doubts, he had signed it, Lionel Grandison said that he had been advised by Dr. Curphey to do so as the "death had been determined to be a suicide by the Suicide Squad." Grandison mentioned that he had been called into the County Coroner's office and handed the document for his signature.

He had felt that he was being pressured into signing it, not an overt pressure but the silent force which superiors can bring to bear on a subordinate, especially a very young and impressionable subordinate. Grandison told Slatzer why he'd been reluctant to affix his name to the paper that officially sealed Marilyn's death: "I felt there had not been enough investigation into the case. There were two or three different police reports that were filed with the Coroner at that time, and there's no way in the world that I, as the signer of that certificate, could have made that determination because the facts were not all in." He mentioned to Slatzer having seen bruises on Marilyn's lifeless skin, and that the name of Bobby Kennedy was much in the air at the office within the first twenty-four hours of receiving Marilyn's body. He testified to the fact that there had been three autopsy reports circulating around the office, one listing "suicide," the next "possible suicide," and last one marked "probable suicide."

These statements were not at odds with the results of my own investigation, nor did his recollections materially affect the case except to throw several unexpected sidelights on it. One of these added yet another issue to Marilyn's mysterious death. It concerned the avid interest of the "insurance people" in Marilyn's "suicide" determination. I had never heard this mentioned before in connection with the circumstances surrounding the "incomplete" autopsy report.

Lionel Grandison had been in the Coroner's office for about two-and-a-half years when he received routine notice from the police that a famous movie star had been found dead under unusual circumstances; he followed up just as he would have with any other corpse by having the body brought to the Hall of Justice, where the County Coroner had his office. Lionel Grandison was very young at the time—about twenty-one—and suddenly he found himself in a place where lots of things were happening. Marilyn Monroe was one of the most famous people in the world and the Coroner's Office in the old downtown Hall of Justice became quite an exciting place for some time. He was receiving, by his count, thirty to forty calls a day from people making inquiries concerning the determination of the cause of death. Newspapermen kept pressing him to learn if there was going to be an investigation, unaware, apparently, that he had no "discretionary responsibility."

Because he was young, there were a lot of circumstances Lionel Grandison at first did not understand. For instance, there was a lot of viewing of the body. Coroner staffers, Hall of Justice employees, police officials, studio people, insurance representatives, high officials from different county departments all filed by Marilyn's crypt, and as a result Lionel Grandison picked up a lot of information. He noticed how the "insurance people" hovered around Crypt 33, which contained the remains of the actress. He told Slatzer that it was not unusual to see people from insurance companies on the premises. They were on a friendly footing with the office personnel. During the holiday season, Grandison said, the insurance people, along with morticians, swooped down on the crypts with cases of liquor and gift-wrapped boxes for everyone in the Coroner's office, from deputy aides to the medical examiners and supervisory personnel.

While the famous body lay in the Coroner's cold-storage vault, Grandison had frequent occasion to talk to representatives from Marilyn's insurance company. The representatives seemed quite anxious to see the death of Marilyn Monroe quickly finalized. They kept pressing the young deputy coroner's aide, who had absolutely no power, to find out when the death certificate was going to be signed and what the determination as to the cause of death was going to be. Grandison understood their haste as perhaps being due to the fear that an inquest might be held. Should it be determined, for example, that Marilyn Monroe had died from a cause other than suicide, the company might have to pay out considerable claims to the deceased's estate.

When, a few days after Marilyn's autopsy, he was called into Dr. Curphey's office, Lionel Grandison found insurance people there. The County Coroner handed him the death certificate to sign. Signing the death certificate of America's greatest celebrity impressed Lionel Grandison. Several other people besides the Chief County Coroner looked on. There was a representative from the District Attorney's office. All were quiet and grave.

Young Grandison flourished his pen and set his name to the appropriate box on the document.

"I was told to sign the death certificate," he told my client, "so it could be filed and the case would be taken to a different level."

Chapter Eight

THE POLICE

Bobby's declaration stated that Marilyn went into a violent fit, screaming "I'm tired of being passed around like a piece of meat!"

Jack Quinn today remains a mystery man. But one thing about him was not a mystery. He knew what happened the day Marilyn died. He knew things that he could not have known except from an official source. From what oracle, except some highly placed person or supersecret document, could he have learned his "inside" knowledge of everything pertaining to the Marilyn Conspiracy? In 1972, he verified facts that had never been published before. He told of matters relating to Marilyn's death known only to my client and myself. On key issues, what he said was proved by later events. He knew so much about the case, about the L.A. Police Department, the Coroner's office, and the Kennedys that it sounded incredible even to our own well-informed ears.

Jack Quinn was not his real name. We never found out his real name. He came from the deep, broke surface, and gasped out his riveting tale. Then he sank back into the murk. We never saw or heard from him again.

One Monday in early August of 1972, Slatzer spent a full day looking for the mysterious informant at the Hall of Records in downtown Los Angeles. He first went to the second floor. Our man was described to disinterested staffers as a male employee in his early forties with slightly gray sideburns, a thick crop of curly dark hair, and tanned skin. When my client had last seen him, the previous Friday, Jack Quinn was wearing brown horn-rimmed glasses, a short-sleeved shirt and matching pants. At this one and only meeting with Slatzer, Jack Quinn wore an identification badge such as is required to be worn by all County employees. It not only had his name on it, but also his picture.

Slatzer's search for Quinn that Monday lasted from the time the Hall of Records opened until it closed. No one had ever seen an individual fitting the description provided by my client. The Microfilm Department had no trace of him. The Personnel Department did not show a Jack Quinn listed as working in the building.

It was very strange. If Jack Quinn did not exist, who was the person claiming to be Jack Quinn? Why did he disguise himself behind a phony identification tag? What motive did he have for contacting us? Unlike some informants, he was not angling to sell information. He was not a publicity seeker, eager to inject his own shabby story into world events. He was not like the "clown" who went around claiming he had buried the red diary on a hilltop in Ohio. Jack Quinn preferred to remain anonymous. I did not beleive he was an impostor. Everything he told my client jibed with our own investigative results. He had nothing to gain from contacting Slatzer and revealing supersecret information which did not come to light until much later.

Jack Quinn was for real. He was as real as "Tom," "Bernie," "D.C.", Lionel Grandison, John Miner, "Mr. O," or "Lieb."
Jack Quinn had his facts right.

Just before noon, about a month before I took over the investigation of the Marilyn Monroe case, Bob Slatzer received a telephone call at his Columbia Pictures office. The caller said he was calling from a pay phone, as he could not speak confidentially from the Microfilm Department at the Hall of Records where he was employed. His name was Jack Quinn. He wanted to talk about a column in the Los Angeles *Herald Examiner* that had appeared that morning. The story quoted Slatzer as saying Marilyn Monroe did not commit suicide but had been murdered. Quinn said that, probably as a result of the story, he had received a call just a few hours before in his office at the Hall of Records from somebody on the Board of Supervisors who asked for a particular microfilm concerning Marilyn's death that had been stored away years ago.

At this point, Slatzer switched on his tape recorder. It was a necessary precaution, for his own investigation after ten years had taken a decisive turn. He had received telephoned threats on his life. He had asked for and received police protection. For some time, he'd been going to his office under armed guard. Someone had already roughed up a person who had been mistaken for his publisher, and soon he was to contact me because he feared for his life. Among all the elements of the Marilyn case he narrated to me on the day when Al Stump first brought him to my office, his encounter with the mysterious Jack Quinn gave me most to think about. From the beginning of my investigation, Jack Quinn helped direct my efforts to the source. He showed that, if there was a cover-up, its center of gravity was in the L.A. Police Department.

Slatzer, as an old newspaperman, knew when to keep quiet and when to talk. He limited himself to monosyllabic comments while listening attentively to the voice on the telephone. Occasionally, his pen dashed to a writing pad on his desk.

"You're right about the Coroner's investigation," Jack Quinn resumed, referring to a statement from Slatzer quoted in the morning newspaper. "You're right about the injection." Quinn went on to say, "The injection was in the arterial artery under the arm, a very small pinprick. She had a lot of bruises on her. She had seen Kennedy, you know."

"Which Kennedy?" Slatzer asked.

He had proceeded from cautious, attentive listening to rapt fascination. The Kennedy-Monroe affair was hardly public knowledge.

Quinn said it was Bobby.

"Bobby lied like a bastard," he continued, "and so did the actor. They lied like bastards. Bobby went out to the house to see her, according to the police report. None of this ever came out at the time of the death."

Slatzer presumed that by the "actor" Quinn meant Peter Lawford, Bobby's brother-in-law, whose Santa Monica beach house was well-known as the place where the Kennedys "partied" and met with Marilyn. But he had no idea of any police report other than the official document, which had been the original source of his suspicion and gradual belief in a cover-up. The police report he knew was filled with contradictions as to the time the doctor arrived, the actions of the two doctors and the housekeeper at the death scene, and the statement by Dr. Engelberg that the empty pill bottle was responsible for Marilyn's death. Its glaring inconsistencies were what had prompted Slatzer to launch his own investigation.

What my client had heard or seen of the police investigation in 1962 convinced him that at the very least their investigation was inadequate. Latent fingerprints were not taken, key people were not interviewed, and "probable suicide" was accepted without a proper inquiry into the possibility of other causes of death. To his utter amazement, Slatzer heard Jack Quinn say that there was an original police report that had the *full* investigation, in which key people going back through the ten days preceding Marilyn's death were interviewed. This report consisted of 723 pages that had been boiled down to the 54 pages officially issued.

He explained that when the City went over to computer, a lot of items from the intelligence units of the Police and Sheriff's departments, "packages," as Quinn called them, had ended up in the Hall of Records. That's how the original police report on Marilyn's death got to his section, he added, because the report was "micro'd" before being destroyed. That morning, as the result of the call from the person on the Board of Supervisors, he had pulled out the micro to look at it again. "Bobby was seeing her on Saturday," Quinn said. "It was in the report."

Slatzer had heard numerous accounts about Bobby's visit to Marilyn in the late afternoon of her death day. These sources were mostly people who'd been in proximity to Marilyn during those hours, or else prominent journalists, such as Walter Winchell or Dorothy Kilgallen, with an "inside" track to contacts in sensitive political positions. His good friend Florabel Muir, a noted columnist who was rarely wrong in police matters, told him on the q.t., just a few weeks after

Marilyn's death, that there had been "mighty suspicious goings-on" the day she died and that it appeared Chief Parker of the L.A. Police Department was involved in full-scale "hanky-panky" to suppress evidence involving Bobby's role in the affair. All the more was Slatzer flabbergasted to hear Jack Quinn repeat that evidence of Bobby's part in the affair was being suppressed. Slatzer heard the mysterious stranger cite uncanny evidence of foul play in Marilyn's death known or suspected by only a few. He heard Quinn say that while at Marilyn's house Bobby Kennedy had a physician with him who, when Marilyn got hysterical during an argument with Bobby, "hit" her with phenobarbital. The official 54-page report issued by the police, Quinn said, was a "joke." He insisted that there was a massive cover-up in both the L.A. Police Department and the Coroner's office.

While listening to the mystery caller, Slatzer wondered about his motives. It was obvious that he had access to startling intelligence on the case. My client got the impression of someone normally cautious and deliberate, the model employee who "covers" himself in everything he does, but for once in his life wants to come forward and tell the truth. Maybe he's fed up with the "dirty business" of covering up, or maybe he simply covets the job of his superior. Some of the big breaks I've had in investigations came from people who were angry with a boss, or who simply disliked their work. This informant gives away secrets because he hates his job or his supervisor. He may even hate the secrets he's supposed to be keeping. Jack Quinn might well be a noble-minded servant of the truth, a "whistleblower" from moral convictions, or a disgruntled employee who could be working in any of the County departments, such as the Coroner's office,

Police or District Attorney's office, that had something to do with the Marilyn case.

Meanwhile, Slatzer felt like a treasure hunter who'd found his cache and is anxious to "secure" it at once. He learned from Quinn that the information was stored on two reels of Olivetti microfilm. When this is copied, it is enlarged with a high-speed copier on special photographic emulsion stock that works only with this particular machine. A ream of paper and the whole job of copying would come to about $30. My client suggested that they meet for lunch and make arrangements for Quinn to copy the microfilm that same afternoon. The informant agreed to meet Slatzer in Hollywood at a deli on Wilcox and Hollywood Boulevard. My client quickly called a friend, photographer Wilson Hong, to witness the conversation.

Quinn showed up a few minutes after Slatzer took a seat and Hong sat down in an adjacent booth. He immediately got down to brass tacks, saying he was on his lunch hour. While talking, he sketched on a note pad a series of blocks. There were seven of them, each representing a portion of the secret police report.

He was a methodical man, with a penchant for explaining things in "flow-chart" style. As he spoke, he drew lines radiating from the boxes, establishing schematic links between the different parts of the 723 pages on microfilm. "The first portion," Quinn said, pointing to the top box on his pad, "goes into the area of general responsibility." The second deals with the investigation report of the L.A. Police Department; the third with the County Sheriff's investigation. The fourth was perhaps the most interesting, Slatzer thought.

He had barely touched his food, so absorbed was he in the startling revelations from the methodical stranger. Taking rapid notes on his writing block, my client learned that the fourth section contained memos and correspondence from all department heads back and forth to each other, such as letters from the police commissioner to the Coroner's office and other law enforcement agencies involved. Some information in this section overlapped with that in the following section, which included reports from a high L.A. Police Department official, a member of the investigation team who appeared to have gone to Washington to get Attorney General Robert Kennedy's personal statement.

"These pages," Quinn said, "might incriminate John Kennedy, who was then president of the United States. There were several memos found in her bedroom, slips of paper, and phone numbers that she'd been calling that day. Quite a few papers were scattered around and all of them were microfilmed."

According to Quinn, Robert Kennedy's statement was allegedly taken in 1962, right after Marilyn's death, with the Attorney General personally initialing the top and bottom of each page and signing under oath. But the reason for Bobby's presence at Marilyn's house, as stated in the file secreted in the Hall of Records, differed from what Slatzer himself and much of Hollywood knew to be the facts of the matter. Quinn said that the police report quoted Robert Kennedy as having come to Los Angeles on August 4 to talk to Marilyn Monroe on behalf of his brother, because Marilyn was "bugging him." Here Quinn obviously meant not electronic eavesdropping but harassment by telephoning the White House. Quinn said that Bobby's statement to the police indicated that Marilyn's behavior had caused serious marital problems for the president, including talk of a divorce between JFK and First Lady Jackie. If the file existed and Quinn was quoting it correctly, Robert Kennedy clearly concealed his own role in the affair, for everyone knew that, in the summer of 1962, Marilyn's involvement had been with him and not with his brother.

The informant continued to describe what, according to the police report, happened at Marilyn's house during Bobby's visit. The high-ranking L.A. Police Department official who took down Bobby's statement, Quinn said, noted that the Attorney General had been painfully honest in his testimony. Quinn himself believed that Bobby had volunteered the surprisingly frank detail in order to guarantee that the record would never be opened. It was simply too embarrassing to a lot of people and not just the Kennedy brothers. It cast the government in a light that was not likely to inspire respect for the presidency.

In Bobby's deposition recorded in the original police report, according to Quinn, Bobby Kennedy said that he and his brother-in-law, Peter Lawford, were at Marilyn's house when she got hysterical, and a doctor had to be summoned to calm her down. Bobby's declaration stated that Marilyn went into a violent fit, screaming "I'm tired of being passed around like a piece of meat." Bobby stated that Marilyn had lunged at him, Quinn said, clawing and screaming that she was called over to Lawford's house at times when they had prostitutes there and that she was "tired of the whole damn mess." It's also on record, Quinn indicated, that Dr. Greenson came to the house around 5:30 P.M. The secret microfilm records Dr. Greenson as having given Marilyn a shot, the informant said, which Bobby Kennedy in his deposition indicated to have been under her left arm. Dr. Greenson apparently did not say what drug was in the shot nor where he gave the injection, but Bobby even named the artery, Quinn added, as well as the name of the drug, pentobarbital, that went into her body.

Section six, Quinn went on to explain, was really in two parts, so you might call the second part section seven, although it should be considered as an extension of the preceding material. Part one dealt with the autopsy, while part two consisted of thirty-two photos of Marilyn's body. Slatzer was eager to have the whole shebang, no matter the cost. At this point, Quinn could have named his price and my client would have gladly given it. He dug into his pocket and pulled out his wallet.

Only in retrospect, after our search had proved fruitless and the mysterious stranger had vanished, did Slatzer understand the awkwardness that ended their meeting. The entire secret report was on two reels, and they were agreed that the whole job would cost about $30. However, to be on the safe side, Slatzer had passed over to Quinn $35. With that, he'd pick up the special photographic emulsion stock that worked only on the Olivetti machine, run off the copies that afternoon and meet Slatzer again that same evening. It was all arranged and they were about to leave the crowded deli. But Quinn was reluctant to accept the money. Slatzer insisted, and at last Quinn with obvious embarrassment pocketed it. My client realized only later the enormous predicament in which he'd put a disgruntled but otherwise honest employee by giving him money for a job he had no intention of performing. Already, I suppose, having revealed his secrets, Jack Quinn regretted his rash act and grew fearful of the hot water he might land himself in if he went further.

Bob Slatzer was to meet Jack Quinn at 6:00 P.M. at

the Smoke House, a restaurant near Warner Brothers studios in North Hollywood. Slatzer sat at the bar. Again his patient friend Wilson Hong sat as witness at an adjacent table, but as an hour crept by, and then another, it became apparent that there would be nothing for him to "witness."

The strange phenomenon of Jack Quinn may be believed or disbelieved. I happen to believe in his authenticity. He simply knew too much. Though not all he knew was accurate, he was correct in some essential points. The doctor with the "medical bag" was seen by the card-playing ladies of Helena Drive at about the time Quinn mentioned to my client. The most startling piece of information was that Bobby Kennedy's visit to Los Angeles on Marilyn's death day was well-known to law enforcement authorities. These included L.A. Police Chief William Parker, Chief of Detectives Thad Brown and Sgt. Clemmons of the West L.A. Police Station. I would come to learn that some of the most important secrets of Marilyn's death were locked away and buried in the unlikeliest of places. This turned my focus to the very bastion guarding those secrets, the L.A. Police Department.

Some of the first things that struck me were certain peculiarities in the original police investigation. From the very beginning, except for the lone voice of Sgt. Clemmons, the police had seemed determined to ignore the possibility of homicide in Marilyn's death. Yet Marilyn Monroe was well-known to law enforcement agencies because she moved in many worlds and, being the "superstar" of her day, met people in the highest circles, attending even semidiplomatic functions, such as meeting Premier Krushchev of the Soviet Union or Indonesian President Sukarno. The

Attorney General, as the top law enforcement official in the country, had a special relationship with the law enforcement agencies in big cities, such as New York, Chicago and Los Angeles. In the latter city, Bobby Kennedy was friends with top officials in the department, where it was common knowledge that Bobby and Marilyn were having an affair. The police and the FBI also knew that Marilyn frequented the underworld, that she was a frequent guest at Frank Sinatra's Cal-Neva Lodge. As well, in her crowded existence, Marilyn had links to left-wing circles through Arthur Miller, becoming widely known for her support of her husband's battle with McCarthyism. As a result, Marilyn was the subject of numerous CIA and FBI reports, well preceding the L.A. Police Department's own 1962 investigation into her death. The mysterious demise of a star of such great notoriety, whose path crossed the paths of so many others, should have aroused the suspicion of the police investigators. They should have realized that Marilyn Monroe knew many people with different motives for silencing her. Simply *because* she was Marilyn Monroe, her death should not have been treated as an ordinary death.

It is perhaps remarkable that until recently our probe managed to obtain more information from the FBI, albeit mostly censored, than from the L.A. Police Department. It was not until 1985, for instance, that we learned, after our repeated requests had been met with repeated denials, that ten years earlier the L.A. Police Department had actually conducted a confidential internal study of Marilyn's death, in which for the first time—thirteen years after the event—Peter Lawford was interviewed. This 1975 internal study, meant for private police consumption only, was finally revealed because of pressure from a national network, ABC. Slatzer discovered that both he and Marilyn Monroe had been subjects, among others, of the study. In 1982, the D.A. managed to pry out of the Police Department the secret of Marilyn's vanished telephone records. But until then, no statement of any kind, other than the original report, was ever released by the L.A. Police Department, despite numerous requests from writers, reporters and investigators. It seemed as if the Police Department believed the files on Marilyn Monroe to have some magical value. Chief Parker kept personal possession of Marilyn's telephone records until his death in 1966, after which the records were squirreled away elsewhere. They were not found until the D.A.'s investigators were supplied them by the L.A. Police Department in 1982. The only police files remaining from the original 1962 Marilyn investigation did not come from the Police Department; they were discovered at the home of the deceased former Chief of Detectives, Thad Brown.

The main problem in obtaining information from the police, or for that matter from any investigative body in Los Angeles that covered the Marilyn death, was that every decade or so the files were routinely purged, and such a purge had been carried out shortly before I began my investigation. Thus, since for many years access to information relating to our probe had been blocked in the L.A. Police Department, we concentrated on getting the FBI files on Marilyn Monroe through the Freedom of Information Act.

The noble-sounding title of this piece of legislation should not be taken literally, since to get anything through it requires a lot of time, patience and perseverance. Once a petition is filed, the Office of the Associate Attorney General assigns it a case number, and from then on it becomes a waiting game. The forms must be filled out faultlessly; if an "i" isn't dotted, or a space isn't checked, or a signature is not in the correct place, the form is returned, usually after an interval of months, after which the weary process begins anew. If an original request has been denied and an appeal is filed, a confirmation comes back that the appeal is "under advisement." Slatzer and I became the architects of a pattern of requests, one after another, following each denial with an appeal. At last, we received a letter from the Chief of Information, Privacy Acts Branch, Records Management Division, United States Department of Justice. It stated for the first time that Marilyn Monroe had long been the subject of special law enforcement interests. "Please be advised," the letter read, "that references to the late Marilyn Monroe are voluminous." It followed with a request that we narrow the scope of the information we were seeking.

Many months were taken up by this fruitless quibbling before we received a dribble of pages from one file, so heavily censored that more than fifty percent of the investigative material could not be read. There were notations about pages "withheld in their entirety," or "pages deleted with no segregable material for release." But from the little that was made available, we discovered that Marilyn Monroe had been the subject of internal FBI and CIA communications as far back as 1955.

These early reports connected Marilyn to her activities in left-wing political circles. They intensified their focus after Marilyn's romance and marriage to Arthur Miller, one of the few writers powerful enough to openly challenge the probings of McCarthyism. In August 1955, the FBI sent the CIA information concerning Marilyn Monroe based on an informant whose identity still remains confidential as this book goes to press. The information in the report was completely "blacked-out." Nevertheless, these and the more recently obtained FBI documents make it clear that the Bureau followed Marilyn closely, beginning with her flight from Hollywood to New York in the mid-Fifties. The intensity of the FBI scrutiny of Marilyn became so strong during her relationship with Arthur Miller that Walter Winchell was to humorously aver in his column that the government was *not* trying to break up the romance.

The FBI files concerning Marilyn saw another increase in volume after her death, when newspaper coverage pointed the finger at the FBI for not telling all it knew about the case, including the FBI's alleged removal of Marilyn's telephone log. Like the L.A. Police Department it denied having any records of Marilyn's telephone calls connecting her with the Kennedys. One year after Marilyn died, an article in *Photoplay* magazine, filled with heavy innuendo at the Kennedys' romantic involvement with Marilyn, excited FBI interest and prompted it to write a lengthy report which came into my possession.

The FBI, whose boss was Attorney General Robert Kennedy, referred to a series of "clues" laid out in the article titled "One Year Later, Marilyn Monroe's Killer Still at Large!" These "clues," according to the FBI report, were that "the man is happily married and has children; that you can see him in a crowd and reach out and touch him; that he is a great man, famous, known the world over; that people look up to him and consider his wife and children lucky; that he is mentioned almost daily in newspapers and magazines; and that he is considered a 'truly honorable man'!"

The FBI report summarizes the "affair between this man and Miss Monroe," as described in the article. It began, according to this summary, "at the worst time of her life and the best time of his. The alleged man was celebrating his good fortune in reaching a height in his career." . . . The remainder of the article allegedly outlines the end of the romance and Miss Monroe's final efforts to renew the relationship. . . . The article states that Miss Monroe's housekeeper has "vanished" and that her publicity agent, Pat Newcomb, is now working in Washington, D.C. It says her second husband, Joe DiMaggio, is the only one who remains faithful and that the man who killed Miss Monroe is still at large and can never be arrested. But, the article asserts, "Wherever he goes, whatever he touches, whomever he sees, he thinks of Marilyn. His guilt never leaves him; his fear has become his friend."

The report goes on to quote Walter Winchell as claiming in a review of the *Photoplay* article that it practically names the man who "killed" Marilyn Monroe.

Except for the private communications between law enforcement authorities, the actors in the drama that unfolded on Marilyn's death did not again become the subject of official discussion on the FBI level until 1973, when Pulitzer-Prize-winning author Norman Mailer published his highly controversial book, *Marilyn,* in which Mailer suggested FBI complicity in the death of the deceased actress. Mailer's allegations caused shocked disbelief among a great many people, and not just those in government. Noted commentators, such as Mike Wallace and movie critic Pauline Kael, accused Mailer of "unsubstantiated theorizing." Articles in the *New York Times* and *Washington Post,* America's leading newspapers, seemed to imply that

Mailer was engaging in "yellow journalism." The FBI report described Mailer's book as having "embellished" rumors originating on the West Coast concerning an affair between Marilyn Monroe and the Attorney General, Robert Kennedy, and that her death was in some way related to this. It cited the earliest "conspiracy theory," propounded in right-wing activist Frank Capell's 1964 book, *The Strange Death of Marilyn Monroe,* the first to place Robert Kennedy at Marilyn's home on her death day, as being among the "rumors" Mailer repeated in his book, giving them a "bizarre twist."

In *Marilyn,* Norman Mailer suggested that though "possibly" the famous actress took her own life, other possibilities were equally likely. One of his suggestions was that the FBI, the CIA, or the Mafia found it of interest that Robert Kennedy, brother of president John Kennedy, was having an affair with the movie star. Mailer suggested that "right-wing" FBI and CIA agents had a "huge motivation" to murder Marilyn Monroe in order to embarrass the Kennedy family, claiming they were furious with the Kennedys because, following the Bay of Pigs invasion, President Kennedy was moving to limit the power of these agencies and, as the disgruntled agents feared, growing "soft" on Cuba.

"A second allegation," the internal FBI memorandum on Mailer states, "is that in 1962 FBI agents in Los Angeles went to the telephone company in Santa Monica, California, and removed a 'paper tape' of Marilyn Monroe's telephone calls, some of which, according to Mailer, were presumably to the White House or White House staff on the night of her death." The FBI categorically branded this as "false," commenting, "this again appears to be a variation of a spurious charge contained in Capell's 1964 book, in which he alleged that such tapes were in the custody of the Los Angeles Police Department."

The furor caused by Mailer's allegations was the beginning of a rising chorus that had the unforeseen result of prompting the L.A. Police Department to launch an in-house confidential review of the case in 1975. Mailer's charge that the L.A. Police Department was sitting on undisclosed information pertaining to the circumstances of Marilyn's death was followed a year later by Bob Slatzer's contention that the Police Department, in collusion with the Coroner's office, had distorted the evidence in order to protect the Attorney General. A lot of "heat" was suddenly being drawn to the Police Department, especially after Slatzer's request in July, 1974, to the L.A. County Grand Jury, asking for a reinvestigation of Marilyn Monroe's death.

Slatzer's information became the basis of a 1975 article which sparked a lot of questions that could not be readily answered because, it was quickly discovered, there were no files pertaining to the death investigation of Marilyn Monroe. Memos flew back and forth, but as cabinets were ransacked and desks turned inside out, no papers of the original 1962 police investigation were found. The October 1975 issue of Hugh Hefner's *Oui* magazine that caused the uproar within the police walls published charges that Marilyn Monroe was murdered and that the determination of cause of death by suicide was a cover-up by the L.A. County Coroner's office and the Police Department.

The search for the original police files was motivated, in my opinion, as an exercise in "damage control" by preparing an internal report—never meant for outside eyes—addressing the disturbing issues raised by Mailer, Slatzer and the *Oui* article. By then many of the official investigative reports in the L.A. Police Department files had been destroyed after ten years, in accordance with record retention policy. However, most, if not all of the relevant L.A. Police Department reports were found in what police called euphemistically the "private archives" of the deceased Chief of the Detective Bureau, Thad Brown. The "private archives," as it turned out, were really the garage of the residence where Thad Brown lived until he passed away in 1973.

From its original police file of the 1962 investigation, the police thirteen years later reviewed certain surviving documents from Thad Brown's garage. The man who decided which material and information from the original police file would be used was today's L.A. Police Chief, Daryl F. Gates, who by his own admission withheld certain information which he regarded as "not part of the public record." Marilyn's telephone records, found among the police's original Monroe file in Thad Brown's garage, did not become part of the "public record" until seven years later when my press conference stung local authorities into action, resulting in a three-and-a-half-month investigation that miraculously retrieved the logs. Until that moment, the police and District Attorney did not acknowledge that the logs existed.

The astonishing recovery of Marilyn's telephone records did not become public knowledge when they were found in 1975. It would take seven years before the 1982 probe by the District Attorney revealed that Marilyn's toll records covering the period near her death were seized and held by the L.A. Police Chief,

William Parker. The confidential internal investigation conducted by the police in 1975 was not made public until ten years later, ironically by the same man who in 1975 headed up this critical investigation, who has since become L.A. Police Chief. Although at this late date in the Marilyn Conspiracy, it was once again left to Police Chief Gates's discretion as to what should be released to the public from the Marilyn files. I have good reason to believe that, given even the startling revelations contained in the limited release of this once "confidential" police report, they would be overshadowed by information still retained in the department's confidential files.

Essentially, what the 1975 Gates investigation did was to look back at the events of 1962 and, by interviewing people who had not been talked to in 1962 or reinterviewing others, it tried to reconstruct the circumstances around Marilyn's death. When it was released ten years later, it confirmed that what Slatzer's contacts had told him about police irregularities was fact. Slatzer's own "Deep Throat" within the L.A. Police Department, I now believe, was motivated to reveal secret information for the same reason Jack Quinn stepped out of anonymity with a phony badge, or Thad Brown secreted Marilyn documents in his garage. Slatzer's "Deep Throat" and Thad Brown were officers who, for understandable reasons, were not satisfied with the way the investigation into Marilyn's death was being handled within the department and on the highest levels.

The 1975 Gates investigation, and later official statements, confirmed what my client and I had been saying all along. They demonstrated that at a very early date Slatzer had been accurate about the suppression of the police files and the police seizure of Marilyn's telephone records. It confirmed that Sgt. Clemmons's original suspicions of Marilyn's doctors deathbed accounts were justified and that the chief police investigator of Marilyn's death, Sgt. Byron, was equally justified in believing that Mrs. Murray had not been completely candid. The most illuminating part of the 1975 Gates report, however, was that for the first time, Peter Lawford, the most important living witness who was never questioned at the time of Marilyn's death, was finally interviewed.

Sgt. Robert Byron of the West L.A. Police Station, the police detective who took over from Sgt. Clemmons, was the original police investigator into Marilyn's death. His report, the only extant official eyewitness account of the death scene, was among the material recovered thirteen years later from Thad Brown's "private archives." According to internal police documents, which were released in late 1985, summaries of interviews with Detective Byron, who had retired by then, revealed that he interviewed a number of people close to the death scene, including Greenson, Engelberg, "Mickey" Rudin, and Mrs. Eunice Murray. Byron also made an attempt in 1962 to contact Lawford, but was informed by the actor's secretary on August 8, three days after Marilyn died, that Lawford was not available for an interview. In his report, Detective Byron noted: "Mr. Lawford had taken an airplane . . . It is unknown at this time the exact destination; however, his secretary stated that she did expect to hear from him and that she would request that he contact this Department at his earliest convenience."

This contact did not take place until thirteen years

later, when Lawford was finally interviewed at his home at 1006 Cory Avenue, Los Angeles, on October 16, 1975, at 5 o'clock.

The most important part of Lawford's statements on the Marilyn case to police in 1975 was what he left unsaid. He did not mention that Bobby Kennedy had flown from San Francisco to Los Angeles, or that he, Peter Lawford, had worked with Hollywood private eye Freddy Otash, the famed "Mr. O," in an effort to "sanitize" Marilyn's house immediately following her death. He did not mention the role of the Greenson Circle, including "Mickey" Rudin, Dr. Greenson's brother-in-law, in the pre-police activities that sent swarms of people flying through the death bedroom while the nude body of the actress lay "swanlike" on her bed. Nor did Peter Lawford speak to police about Bobby Kennedy's meeting with Marilyn just hours before she died, or that Bobby Kennedy had been at the Beverly Hilton that afternoon. He failed to explain to the officers why it seemed to take the Greenson Circle, particularly the housekeeper, so long to notify police after Marilyn was found dead. Lawford did not bring up to investigators his own efforts to get Marilyn to come to his beach house in order to calm her down after her "fight" with Bobby on the day she died.

When he finally talked "at his earliest convenience," thirteen years later, the story he told police bore major inconsistencies to what he had told the press in 1962, when he said he'd talked to Marilyn on the phone about seven o'clock in the evening to invite her to dinner and that Marilyn had told him she "felt happy and was going to bed." In 1975, this same call was no longer to the cheerful screen star who refuses a dinner date with her friend, but to a "suicide" who at the other end of the line appeared to be literally slipping into death.

In the interview with police, Lawford stated that Marilyn Monroe was a regular guest at his home in Santa Monica those last weeks before she died, and that when he telephoned her at approximately 5:00 P.M. on August 4, it was to ask her if she was coming to his house that weekend. He said she sounded "despondent," and he tried to convince her to forget about her problems and join him and his wife, Pat, for dinner that evening. According to Lawford, Marilyn had said that she would consider it.

About an hour later, according to the interview recorded in the secret 1975 internal police report, Lawford telephoned her a second time to ascertain why she hadn't yet arrived at his home. This time Lawford said she "was still very despondent and her manner of speech was slurred. She stated she was tired," Lawford continued, "and would not be coming. Her voice became less and less audible." Lawford said he then "began to yell at her in an attempt to revive her," describing it as a "verbal slap in the face." Then he heard her say, "Say goodbye to Pat, say goodbye to Jack (JFK) and say goodbye to yourself, because you're a nice guy."

When the phone went dead, Lawford, assuming she had hung up, tried several times to redial her number and received a busy signal each time. He then called his agent to tell him he was going over to Marilyn's house. His agent was Milton Ebbins, and Ebbins, he said, recommended against it. (Lawford remarked, "You know how agents are.") Ebbins suggested he would himself call her doctor or lawyer, and eventually Ebbins was able to reach Mickey Rudin. Lawford stated he had often talked to Marilyn on the phone while she was under the effect of downers, and her voice on this evening sounded about the same as it usually did when she'd taken pills. "For some reason," the confidential police report quotes Lawford, he had a "gut feeling" that something was wrong, and "still blames himself for not going to her home himself."

For the first time, light was also shed on the mysterious weekend referred to in my own file as the "Cal-Neva Incident." As age and excess caught up with Lawford, impairing the old debauchee's health and memory, his account of Marilyn's final hours changed. But in the bare scenario he painted to police of the Cal-Neva Incident, an important episode with far-reaching implications is revealed.

Shortly before her death, Marilyn was at the Cal-Neva, which was then, according to press reports, associated with mobsters, in particular with "boss of bosses" Sam "Momo" Giancana. At the same time, according to the newly found phone records, Marilyn was in touch with the Justice Department. The Cal-Neva Lodge, beautifully situated at Lake Tahoe, was a dangerous place for Marilyn to be at. It represented the crossroads of two worlds. Just as the Cal-Neva Lodge itself physically straddled two statelines, so that one part of the lodge was in California where gambling was prohibited and the other part was in Nevada where gambling was legal, so Marilyn at Cal-Neva moved in the two worlds where the law and the lawless mixed.

She had a longstanding relationship with Frank Sinatra, friend of both the Lawfords and the Kennedys, who had a business interest in Cal-Neva. A longtime Kennedy supporter, Sinatra had been the singer of the presidential campaign theme song. With

Lawford, whom he called "brother-in-law," he formed the much-publicized band of gay-blades-about-town known as the "Rat Pack," whose chief interest was to "party" and provide the president with a good time on his trips to the Coast. Sinatra's on-and-off-again affair with Marilyn dated to the mid-Fifties. According to one recent Marilyn death prober, the famous crooner seemed to maintain many connections that tied him to Marilyn Monroe, through sharing the same psychiatrist, Dr. Greenson, as well as the same lawyer, "Mickey" Rudin. Sinatra reportedly was also good friends with Marilyn's gynecologist and his intimacy with Marilyn lasted throughout her romances with both Kennedys, and ended only with her death.

Around the very period of Marilyn's Cal-Neva visit, however, Sinatra had become the subject of a Justice Department investigation that tied him to the "boss of bosses" in the question of ownership of the lodge. Bobby Kennedy, according to his biographers, was just then distancing the White House from Sinatra and his extensive Palm Springs guarded oasis, where the president had frequently been a guest. Earlier that summer, Bobby had urged JFK to cancel a planned stay at the Sinatra compound on a presidential visit to California. Marilyn Monroe was involved with all three men. It seemed as if her body, in fact, was an instrument of communication between them. In her red diary, Slatzer had seen reference to Bobby's vow to cause Frank Sinatra to lose his Nevada gambling license at Cal-Neva, because of Justice Department allegations that Sinatra maintained unsavory connections in the underworld.

Marilyn's visit to Cal-Neva took place about three weeks before she died. According to the 1975 police interviews with Lawford, Marilyn traveled with the

Lawfords to Cal-Neva in Lake Tahoe where Frank Sinatra was headlining at the time. When Lawford awoke one morning, he stated to police, his wife told him Marilyn had overdosed the evening before. She had been discovered when she fell out of bed and was able to be revived without professional medical assistance. He did not say whether Dr. Greenson had been notified of this serious incident at Cal-Neva; if there had been a suicide attempt, as described by Lawford, Frank Sinatra, who knew Dr. Greenson well, or Lawford himself, must have informed her psychiatrist. Dr. Greenson must have told the Suicide Team about it after Marilyn's death. (Remember, John Miner, the D.A.'s Legal-Medical Head who interviewed Dr. Greenson, rejected the "simple suicide" explanation because of confidential information which he was told by Dr. Greenson thirteen years before). There's never been a satisfactory explanation by any of the witnesses of Marilyn's Cal-Neva Incident—unless she spoke of it on one of the Greenson tapes.

This visit to the secluded resort occurred at about the time Marilyn told Slatzer that Bobby had disconnected the private number he'd given her. Lawford was adamant that there was no connection between RFK, the likely cause of Marilyn's malaise at Cal-Neva, and the screen star. He told his questioners that whenever RFK came to town he would come to the Lawford home and swim in the pool. He also stated that "Miss Monroe was a regular guest at his beach-front home those last weeks before she died." On the crucial question of Marilyn's last days he vehemently denied that the Attorney General was in the Los Angeles area on the fateful weekend of Marilyn's death, and claimed to have no knowledge of Bobby's purported stay in San Francisco during the same period. He told police that charges by Slatzer that Kennedy had been to her house the day she died were "pure fantasy."

Lawford's denials notwithstanding, FBI reports obtained by Kennedy chronicler Arthur Schlesinger put Robert Kennedy definitely in San Francisco that weekend. For Bobby's sister Pat and his brother-in-law Peter, in Santa Monica, not to have known about his presence in the state was simply not credible. The FBI report stated that on August 3–5 "the Attorney General, accompanied by his wife and four children, spent the weekend with Mr. and Mrs. John Bates on their ranch at Gilroy, California. (Gilroy is about 300 miles north of Los Angeles).

Lawford told police that the article published in Hefner's magazine, placing RFK with Marilyn on the day of her death in Los Angeles, was false. He said he had protested to Hefner who told him that he, Hefner, was not aware of the article until after it had been printed. Hefner apologized, according to Lawford, saying had he known of it, the article wouldn't have run.

Lawford's testimony was interesting, even though it was not released until 1985, after Lawford had died, with L.A. Police Chief Gates's 1975 internal police study on Marilyn's death. By the facts then known, nearly a quarter century after the event, it was obvious that Lawford was far from telling all he knew, or even telling that which he did know with any degree of accuracy.

Until the Gates release of confidential documents, there had been no record of witnesses close to Marilyn's death scene. These were known to have been interviewed in 1962 by the original police investigator, Sgt. Robert Byron of the West L.A. Detective Division, the officer who relieved Sgt. Clemmons in the early morning of August 5. Sgt. Byron's attempt to interview Lawford, three days after Marilyn's death, resulted in his discovery that the president's brother-in-law had taken a plane to an "unknown destination," which subsequently turned out to be the Kennedy compound at Hyannisport. Byron also interviewed others close to the death scene, including Dr. Greenson, Dr. Engelberg, Mrs. Eunice Murray, and "Mickey" Rudin. Bryon's original police record remained lost until the 1975 in-house police probers located it in Thad Brown's garage. It became public in the fall of 1985.

The original Byron interviews were conducted for the most part in the days and weeks following Marilyn's death. The two doctors, when interviewed on August 6, the day after Marilyn's autopsy, had by then agreed to a uniform time sequence of their actions, Dr. Greenson stating that Mrs. Murray had called him at 3:30 A.M. because she was unable to get into Marilyn's bedroom and the light was on. He said he had told her to pound on the door and call him back, which she did five minutes later, according to Dr. Greenson, with the report that Marilyn Monroe was lying on the bed with the phone in her hand and "looked strange." Dr. Greenson stated he then told the housekeeper to call Dr. Engelberg, while he himself left for the deceased's residence, where he "broke the window pane," noted Byron, "and entered through the window and removed the phone from her hand." By then, Byron recorded in his report, rigor mortis had set in and at 3:50 A.M. Dr. Engelberg arrived and pronounced Marilyn Monroe dead.

The most important of Byron's notations with reference to this interview was the "time sequence" of the rigor mortis, since it was inconsistent with the accounts given by several other people close to the events that night. Walter Schaefer of the ambulance service told me that one of his ambulances took Marilyn at about 2:00 A.M. of August 5 to the Santa Monica Hospital; there, according to Schaefer, she died, after which her body was returned to her home. It is also inconsistent with the account given by Sgt. Clemmons and Guy and Don Hockett, the father-and-son mortician team who, by Marilyn's advanced state of lividity, believed she had died about six to eight hours earlier. That would put her death at 8:00 P.M. of the evening before, which was about the time Lawford had stated in the secret 1975 police interview that he had heard Marilyn's voice "fading out" on the telephone.

It is easier to make sense of these discrepancies after nearly a quarter century. But it must have been evident to the police in both the "official" Marilyn death probes it conducted, the original one in 1962 and the other in 1975. It must also have been clear to the District Attorney's office when in 1982 it revealed for the first time that Marilyn's missing telephone records were contained in L.A. Police Department files. (The D.A. must have been even more surprised to learn that these lost telephone records did not come from police department vaults but were finally recovered from Thad Brown's suburban home).

In one of the few interviews ever given by Pat Newcomb, Marilyn's agent, who was with her at the house until just a few hours before her mysterious death, an astonishing clue surfaced, a clue that contradicted the accounts given by the two physicians found by Sgt. Clemmons on the death scene. This important clue put into doubt whatever the two doctors might subsequently say, whether about an empty Nembutal bottle or the time of rigor mortis. We cannot rely on the doctors' testimony of the events because they told no one, except perhaps the authors of the secret microfilm report seen by Jack Quinn, that there were other people on the death scene before the police arrived. Pat Newcomb said "Mickey" Rudin, Marilyn's lawyer, called her about 4:00 A.M. to give her the news of Marilyn's death. More than twenty years later, Milton Ebbins, Lawford's agent, also recalled that Rudin had been at Marilyn's house in the early hours of August 5.

Detective Byron interviewed "Mickey" Rudin on August 10, 1962, and noted the following in his report: "Mr. Rudin stated that on the evening of 8-4-62 his exchange received a call at 8:25 P.M. and that this call was relayed to him at 8:30 P.M. The call was for him to call Milton Ebbins. At about 8:45 P.M. he called Mr. Ebbins, who told him that he had received a call from Peter Lawford stating that Mr. Lawford had called Marilyn Monroe at her home and that while Mr. Lawford was talking to her, her voice seemed to 'fade out' and when he attempted to call her back, the line was busy. Mr. Ebbins requested that Mr. Rudin call Miss Monroe and determine if everything was all right, or attempt to reach her doctor. At about 9:00 P.M., Mr. Rudin called Miss Monroe and the phone was answered by Mrs. Murray. He inquired of her as to the physical well-being of Miss Monroe and was assured by Mrs. Murray that Miss Monroe was all right. Believing that Miss Monroe was suffering from one of her despondent moments, Mr. Rudin dismissed the possibility of anything further being wrong."

In my opinion, "Mickey" Rudin, Marilyn's lawyer, was never properly questioned, according ι the newly released 1962 police report, about his role that night. In his professional capacity, he was intimate with the conflicts in her life, and as Dr. Greenson's brother-in-law, he might be expected to be equally familiar with her mental state. Did he know of Lawford's story about her alleged suicide attempt three weeks before at Cal-Neva? Was Rudin aware of the "very important men" who were creating havoc in Marilyn's life, as his psychiatrist brother-in-law had reported to investigators from both the D.A.'s and Coroner's offices?

Later "Mickey" Rudin was to tell columnist Earl Wilson that Marilyn was constantly talking about revising her will, but that he "avoided the subject," apparently believing she was not, according to the legal principle of compos mentis, of "sound mind." "After all," Rudin is quoted as asking Wilson, "was she of sound mind?" Given his knowledge of Marilyn's volatile psychic condition, and Peter Lawford's alarming call that night, I wondered how a high-powered attorney could be satisfied to accept Mrs. Murray's statement at 9:00 P.M. that evening "that Miss Monroe was all right." According to new statements made on the eve of the completion of my own investigation, Rudin must have been far more knowledgeable than is reflected in Sgt. Byron's original 1962 report about the events the night Marilyn died. Byron's report on Rudin was either terribly incomplete or was a deliberate attempt to distort the facts concerning Marilyn's demise. (According to the Hocketts and Walter Schaefer, as well as pathologists consulted, she must have been dead by the time Rudin first called).

Sgt. Byron also talked to Mrs. Murray, who again stated that during the evening of August 4 at about 7:30 P.M., about the time Lawford reported Marilyn's voice as "fading out," she overheard Marilyn talking on the telephone to Joe DiMaggio Jr., and, Byron notes, "from the tone of Miss Monroe's voice, she believed her to be in very good spirits." The housekeeper told the investigator from the West L.A. Police Station that Rudin called her about 9 P.M. to inquire about Marilyn, but "Mr. Rudin did not talk to Miss Monroe," Byron quoted Mrs. Murray.

In the conclusion of his report, the detective made a significant remark that should have sparked further interviews of Mrs. Murray, if not the launching of a full-scale police investigation. It echoed the report by the first outsider to reach Marilyn's bedroom, Sgt. Clemmons. In a special "note" attached to his report, the detective wrote: "It is this officer's opinion that Mrs. Murray was vague and possibly evasive in answering questions pertaining to the activities of Miss Monroe during this time. It is not known whether this is or is not intentional."

The police handling of the investigation in the days immediately following Marilyn's death was at the time a subject of great interest to two longstanding friends of my client, the noted columnists Walter Winchell and Florabel Muir. Their names were familiar to every newspaper reader. Winchell had informants in the highest places in Washington, while Muir specialized in police contacts. She was a close personal friend of Police Chief Parker.

At first, it appeared that the police investigation would result in a Grand Jury inquest. On August 7, two days following Marilyn's death, investigators in press conference after press conference stated their commitment to interview "anybody and everybody." The *Los Angeles Times* and the *New York Herald Tribune* had headline stories questioning the causes of

Marilyn's demise. But within the immediate days that followed, something strange and unexplainable happened to suffocate the efforts of police and Coroner officials. One week following Marilyn's autopsy, Florabel Muir informed her readers that "strange pressures are being put on the L.A. Police. . . . Sources close to the probers said tonight . . . the purported pressures are mysterious. They apparently are coming from persons who had been closely in touch with Marilyn the past few weeks." She also wrote, "The police have impounded the telephone company's taped record of those (Marilyn's) outgoing calls." Five days later, the District Attorney, the Chief Coroner, and Police Chief Parker closed the case for good.

Politics may have affected the D.A.'s seeming haste to bury this very touchy issue, but the abrupt about-face was one of the factors responsible for our dogged determination to complete the investigation into the shrouded circumstances of Marilyn's death. Through his reading of the red diary, Bob Slatzer knew better than most the dangerous worlds in which Marilyn had become embroiled. It came as a shock to him when he heard the news that the D.A. had closed the case without any real inquiry into the circumstances of her death.

In his own investigation, Florabel's information represented an important "clue," that the key to the cover-up puzzle was to be found in the L.A. Police Department and in the information in Marilyn's final phone records; and for the first time I can report in print what for years I've held in professional confidence, namely, that the source of some of my client's inside information from the L.A. Police Department was Chief Parker himself, who communicated in "confidence" to Florabel Muir, who in turn communicated this "in confidence" to my client Bob Slatzer, who in turn communicated Parker's "in confidence" opinions and statements to me when I first took over the case.

Florabel Muir told Bob the incredible story of the Parker-Kennedy connection that resulted in the case being "covered up" at the source. While officially the police department did nothing to conduct a criminal investigation into the facts behind Marilyn's death, it actually ran an intelligence operation which to this day remains a police "top secret." For reasons never fully explained by investigators in the District Attorney's office, this special division within the police department, reporting only to Chief Parker, among other things, seized Marilyn's phone records as part of an operation obviously aimed at concealing sensitive information regarding Kennedy's involvement. Florabel Muir provided this important tip, which indicated to Slatzer the shape of a cover-up of Marilyn's death. Muir told Slatzer that during a visit with Chief Parker, he had boastfully "flashed" Marilyn's telephone records in front of her eyes, bragging, "they're my ticket to get Hoover's job when Bobby Kennedy becomes president."

Shortly after learning this astounding news from Muir, Slatzer began paying a series of visits to the L.A. Police Department to determine what had become of Marilyn's final telephone records. One day, unannounced, he confronted Chief Parker as he was coming out of his office on his way to lunch. Slatzer shocked the bespectacled Parker by directly confronting him and requesting a meeting to discuss Marilyn Monroe's missing telephone records. Parker did a double take, according to Slatzer, and said he "didn't have any information on that subject."

"But I've heard you have Marilyn's records in your office," Slatzer pressed the Chief.

"Just who in the hell are you?" Parker shouted, flushing bright pink.

"Just a friend. My name's Bob Slatzer."

"A friend of whom?"

"Marilyn Monroe."

The Chief immediately turned around, shouting scornfully over his shoulder as he retreated down the hall. "Well, somebody's given you a bum steer. I don't know what you're talking about."

Meanwhile, Captain James Hamilton, head of the L.A. Police Department Intelligence Division, personally directed an ongoing clandestine Monroe investigation for Chief Parker. Tom Reddin, Chief Parker's successor, witnessed the events of the original 1962 Marilyn probe. Reddin has stated that during Hamilton's Intelligence Division investigation it was a matter of common knowledge at the department that Marilyn had a relationship with the Kennedys. On Captain Hamilton's role in the Monroe investigation, Reddin has stated to independent investigators, "Hamilton talked to only two people, God and Chief Parker." Reddin also said that he was aware of an internal document that never became public. This practically corroborated Jack Quinn's claim that the secret 723-page L.A. Police Department Marilyn Monroe report actually existed.

For the first time, in 1984, a *Los Angeles Times* correspondent revealed what I have since corroborated independently and now report, namely, that Hamilton had personally told him of having had the telephone history "of the last day or two of Marilyn Monroe's life." But my own investigation has revealed that Captain Hamilton and Chief Parker had much more.

Both the District Attorney and the Police Department had known in 1962 what my investigation took twenty-three years to uncover, that at the time of Marilyn's death she had been calling Bobby Kennedy, then the Attorney General, in Washington, D.C., on a regular basis, and that Police Chief Parker had seized these telephone records and used them for personal political objectives. Also, that it was known to Chief Parker and others, including the District Attorney, that Robert Kennedy was in Los Angeles and was seen in Beverly Hills on Marilyn's death night. I learned from Deputy D.A. "Mike" Carroll, who conducted the 1982 District Attorney's investigation, and I here report for the first time, that the Deputy D.A. assigned to the Marilyn case in 1962, John Dickie, had told Carroll that a "secret investigation of Marilyn's death had found that RFK had been at the Beverly Hilton on the day of her death." In 1985, the *Los Angeles Times* tried to interview Dickie on Carroll's claim of what Dickie had told him. Dickie refused.

My own investigation has revealed that it was common knowledge on all levels of the police department that RFK was in L.A. the weekend of Marilyn's death, as the mysterious Jack Quinn revealed to my client in the Hollywood deli. The Chief of Detectives at the time, Thad Brown, who himself expressed the belief before his own death in 1973 that Kennedy and Lawford were together in Los Angeles on Marilyn's last night, was the only one to preserve any evidence from the 1962 police investigation, including Marilyn's phone records, which he stored—against official policy—for years in his suburban garage. Thad Brown undoubtedly took this action, at least in part, because he was critical of Chief Parker's muzzling of the investigation. Finis Brown, Thad's brother, has confirmed these findings. Finis said Thad Brown had actually conducted an unofficial investigation of his own. Sgt. Clemmons, who was the first to insist that Marilyn had been murdered, also believed that Bobby was in Los Angeles that weekend. Clemmons had learned these facts from his own investigation inside the police department. As a result of making this belief vocal, he was cautioned by Parker to be quiet. Parker was known to run the department with an iron hand. When Clemmons made his views known, he soon found himself unceremoniously dropped from the force.

In 1966, when Marilyn's death records were still in police files, L.A. Mayor Sam Yorty joined the legion of unofficial investigators when, in the aftermath of Chief Parker's death, he asked for Marilyn's file to be sent to him. He recalled having been told before by Chief Parker that Kennedy was in town on the weekend Marilyn died. "Chief Parker told me that he knew Bobby Kennedy was at the Hilton Hotel the night she died, and he (Kennedy) was supposed to be in Fresno." Yorty remembers, "I don't think there is any police department file on that. I think the Chief kept the file separately. As mayor, I sent for it later when the Chief died, and they didn't have it."

Chapter Nine

THE WIRETAPPERS

"He said that Marilyn was dead and 'they got Bobby out of the city and back to Northern California'."

In the last weeks of her life, Marilyn Monroe became paranoid about her phones being tapped. She'd even begun carrying a bag of coins for more "sensitive" calls, which were placed from pay phones. How did she know her phones were tapped? I always wondered. Possibly she assumed that, with her red diary and her affairs with "very important men," there were people in various places keenly interested in her movements. She appeared to be convinced the "tapping business" had some connection with Bobby. It's possible, in my opinion, it had something to do with Cal-Neva, where she might have been given a "message." Marilyn probably figured it had something to do with Bobby, because of the crushing awareness that she was important only in relation to the "important men" in her life. But whatever Marilyn's reasoning might have been, she was correct: her house was wired from

198

top to bottom, inside and out, in the inimitable manner of Hoffa wireman, "Bernie" Spindel, who did not even omit to install a bug in her bathroom.

Obviously, those who wished to get the tapes on the Kennedy-Monroe affair had a motive. Several competing parties were embroiled with each other and with Marilyn at the time. All had a motive to get the tapes either to embarrass Bobby or to destroy him. For years Bob Slatzer and I have searched for these critically important Kennedy-Monroe tapes, which I believe would point the finger at the parties who benefited most from Marilyn's murder. Marilyn's knowledge of important national security secrets, including the Byzantine interrelation between the state, organized crime and government intelligence services, made her a natural target for monitoring her voice and eventually silencing it. It was my incredible encounter with "Tom" which finally convinced me of the facts which, I believe, would prove, if properly investigated, why Marilyn was murdered.

I talked to "Tom" in August, 1982, exactly twenty years after Marilyn died in her Brentwood home. He called me up and without introducing himself said, "I was involved in something in the past that you are receiving a lot of notoriety about; I have some information that just might help you."

At this point I switched on the tape, the same tape which a few months later was to stun into silence the triumvirate of the D.A.'s Marilyn investigation, Carroll, Tomich and Anderson. "Tom" was like Watergate's "Deep Throat," a "hearsay" witness. I played the tape at that time for Carroll not because I expected him to accept "hearsay" as evidence. All I wanted was for him to hear what had been buzzing through the electronic surveillance wires for years. "Tom" did not speak in riddles. He shot straight from the hip. "I was a key man in Spindel's organization," he announced on the tape. His employer in the early Sixties, he said, was B.R. Fox, the name which I already knew to belong to Spindel's clandestine eavesdropping firm.

"Tom" went over his whole background with me. He said he was an electronics engineer, responsible for designing many of Spindel's bugs. "Marilyn's phones were definitely tapped," he told me. "So were all the rooms of her house." My anonymous informant seemed to be a phlegmatic type, and I think he called me because he was proud to talk of the equipment he'd worked on for Spindel. When he mentioned the type of equipment used to bug Marilyn, he became enthusiastic. "We used the lower aircraft band, 112–115 mg." the former Spindel wireman explained. "It was a clear band, not monitored, seldom used."

It became apparent as I listened that I was talking to a pro of top caliber, a technician who delights in intricate devices and the perfection of "equipment." The bug planted at Marilyn's house, he explained, was not a crystal frequency, the kind commonly used in that era, but a VOX, a new technique at the time that was voice-activated and capable of stopping the recorder when there were no audible sounds or voices. This saved reels of blank tape, not to mention eliminating hours of monitoring time. "Tom" then told me what could be heard on the Kennedy-Monroe tapes obtained by his employer Spindel of the B. R. Fox Company.

"Marilyn was slapped around. You could actually hear her being slapped, even hear her body fall to the floor. You could hear her hit the deck, and all the sounds that took place in her house that night." One of the men said, according to "Tom": "What do we do with her body now?"

No one has confessed to the murder of Marilyn Monroe. No one is likely to. But if Spindel's Kennedy-Monroe tapes are recovered, though not "admissible" as evidence under the current statutes of law, the voices on them will serve as a confession. During our investigation, we had numerous contacts with sources who, long before "Tom," verified that Marilyn's house had been bugged. We knew who ordered the bugs that were put in her phones and all over the rest of her house.

"Bernie Spindel was Jimmy Hoffa's personal man," "Tom" told me. "And you had better believe he had a good tap on her house."

"You can say that in all truthfulness?" I asked.

"Tom" insisted, "I tell you it's a fact right now. The tapes will tell you everything you want to hear and maybe a little bit more. The hell with the diary. The tapes are what you really want; the voices of the killers are right there."

"Who has the tapes?" I asked.

I knew "Bernie" had died just after he was let out of a New York prison and that he was hardly the type to have left detailed instructions as to the location of the Kennedy-Monroe tapes. It was more likely that he would entrust them to one of his loyal followers. My informant then mentioned the name of the man who had at least one of the original Spindel/Hoffa tapes or else a copy.

His name cannot now be revealed, so I shall identify him as "D.C.," since he lives in Washington. "Tom" told me that he and "D.C." had formerly been high-ranking officials in the Spindel organization. In addition to conventional "bugging," both were involved in manufacturing assassination devices for the CIA. They also instructed local and federal law enforcement agents on bugging and debugging.

In the old days, "Tom" reminisced, he and "D.C." had had a lab in Alexandria, Virginia, and two fronts were created: one in the Watergate complex and the second one off Pennsylvania Avenue right near the White House. "We were cooking at full steam," my informant remembered.

I asked "Tom" why "D.C." had kept the tapes all these years. My informant replied that it was because "D.C." wanted to "protect Bernie."

In the early morning of December 16, 1966, a caravan of marked and unmarked New York State Police cars pulled into the driveway of Spindel's home in Holmes, New York. The raid was ordered by the New York County District Attorney, and it resulted in Spindel being accused of unlawful possession of equipment belonging to the telephone company. During the raid, the D.A.'s men confiscated all of Spindel's most sensitive tapes and files, which, according to the Spindels, included the highly explosive Kennedy-Monroe tapes. It was Mrs. Spindel who poignantly summarized the reasons behind the bugging of Marilyn and the turbulent political conditions in which Marilyn had become the center of a deadly concern. Startlingly, Mrs. Spindel suggested that Marilyn might even have known and have participated in the making of these dangerous tapes.

"Marilyn was a very frightened woman," Mrs. Spindel said, "and I think she had reason to be. It's possible that she made those tapes herself, or that she had Bernie do it for her. There was so much going on then. The assassination attempts against Castro—all that stuff with Giancana and Sinatra, the Kennedys' affairs . . . the Hoffa feud . . . I think Marilyn was afraid for her life. And, of course, Bernie was right in the middle of it.''

Mrs. Spindel's revelations, corroborated by "Tom," proved that the notorious "Bernie" Spindel's wiretapping of Marilyn's house was almost certainly performed at the behest of one of two groups—Organized Crime or Jimmy Hoffa, because both at the time were archenemies of Marilyn's secret paramour, who was also the Attorney General, the nation's chief cop. Both were desperately trying to get something on Bobby to blackmail him.

It was another private detective, Freddy Otash, the noted Hollywood private eye known in the field as "Mr. O," a name as legendary as "Bernie," who was to finally reveal Spindel's electronic dirty tricks. A Hollywood status symbol like the Hollywood psychiatrist, Otash had many noted Hollywood celebrities as clients, including Howard Hughes, Errol Flynn, Lana Turner, Judy Garland, as well as Peter Lawford and Frank Sinatra.

In fact, Otash's name was linked to Sinatra in his most widely publicized assignment, the case involving DiMaggio and Sinatra's "Wrong Door Raid" on Marilyn some years before her death. It was only natural that the two men who connected the wires for famous clients would each know what the other was doing.

In 1983, for the first time Otash told an interviewer the incredible spy vs. spy high-stakes contest that developed between him and Spindel over Marilyn's "bugging." "I was contacted by Bernard Spindel on behalf of Jimmy Hoffa"; but he also told the interviewer that he would have nothing to do with it and that it was his understanding that Spindel did come out to the West Coast and "hit" Marilyn's phones. "There was a room bug, too—it wasn't just the phones."

Ironically, it was Otash who would run an operation to electronically "sweep" the bedroom for another one of the interest groups warring to exercise control over Marilyn—a war that continued even after her death. In 1985, just as my probe was creating a fresh sensation, "Mr. O" broke his silence on the Marilyn case. For the first time, he told of his role in what happened at 12305 Fifth Helena Drive the night Marilyn died.

When Freddy Otash was asked in 1983 by a Marilyn investigator about hearsay allegations concerning his role with Peter Lawford and Bobby Kennedy, he turned away the interviewewer's question. will neither confirm nor deny it." He told the interviewer that to corroborate the accounts which placed him in the position of Peter Lawford's chief security man that night would cause him "to end up in front of a Grand Jury." But in 1985, amidst a flurry of fresh Marilyn interest, he told of being telephoned late that night by Lawford and of a conversation in which Lawford admitted that he and Bobby had already known that Marilyn was dead, shortly after midnight, hours before police were called.

Lawford called Otash to employ his services on a midnight mission to "sanitize" Marilyn's house the night of August 4–5. With Lawford busy hustling Bobby out of town, he needed Otash to go to the house and remove anything incriminating. Lawford said, Otash recalled, that he (Lawford) had just left Monroe and that Bobby had been there earlier. "He said," Otash continued, "that Marilyn was dead and 'they got Bobby out of the city and back to Northern California.' "

Otash has been described as the "quintessential private eye"—hard-drinking, street smart and tough. After Lawford's call to him that night, they met at the detective's Hollywood office at about 2:00 A.M.; Lawford, according to Otash, looked "half-crocked and half-nervous."

Lawford, according to the legendary "Mr. O," described what he had done at the death scene: "I took what I could find and I destroyed it—period." Otash said Lawford complained, "I'm so out of it," saying he'd feel better if Otash went to the death scene to pick up anything that had escaped Lawford's sweep. Lawford meant only one thing. He needed Otash to "clean out" Spindel's electronic ears.

Otash refused. "I'm not going out there."

It was too touchy, even for "Mr. O," who had himself once worked for Jimmy Hoffa and other famous mob figures, as well as for Hollywood celebrities. Otash could, with his knowledge of the law and the backing of sound legal counsel, venture out in this blank atmosphere where the silence was broken by the "tap," audible only to the highly trained wireman's ear. He had knowledge of the no-man's land where two worlds meet and borders are not precisely defined; it was his natural terrain, but the Monroe's wired home fell outside it. Too touchy, even for the legendary "Mr. O."

Otash was perhaps the only person in Los Angeles who knew how the death scene was connected by Spindel's wires to the ears of powerful and easily irritable people. "First," he told Lawford, explaining why he wouldn't go to Marilyn's house, "I'm too well known."

Otash said he then called one of his operatives, a skilled installer of listening devices, someone probably much like "Tom," I imagine, someone in love with his "equipment" who needs silence and quiet and anonymity to do his best. Otash's secret wireman apparently made his unobtrusive entry onto the death scene at Marilyn's Spanish-style home, but found working conditions there next to impossible, according to Otash. Hollywood's tough private eye, like Walt Schaefer of the ambulance service, knew that a lot of Hollywood stories just never got told. Finally, in 1985, he told it as it was: "When they got there, from what they tell me, the place was swarming with people. They were incapable of sweeping the place or anything."

Lawford had earlier told Otash of the events preceding the commotion that prevented Otash's wireman from conducting a sweep to remove the Spindel bugs. This corroborated what Marilyn had confided to Slatzer in the summer of 1962. I remembered the picture Slatzer had painted in wistful words—Marilyn Monroe radiating the glow of a happiness that turned out to be false, greeting Slatzer excitedly, exulting, "Bobby Kennedy has promised to marry me! What do you think of that?"

Otash said Lawford had told him Bobby and Marilyn had had a fight over their relationship—whether he was going to marry her—and "he (Bobby) left Marilyn's house."

Otash recalled Lawford telling him that Bobby had found Marilyn "ranting and raving," with Bobby expressing concern "over what may come out of this." Then Lawford had spoken with her and she had said to him that she was "passed around like a piece of meat," and that she had had it, and didn't want Bobby to "use" her anymore. "She called the White House," Lawford told Otash, "and there was no response from the president. She was told he was in Hyannisport and she didn't connect with him. She kept trying to get him."

Otash is retired now and speaks by telephone from France. His career as celebrity wireman has been laid aside. He walks the beach at Cannes, where he lives, and sits at one of the cafés that looks out over the waterfront with its elegant sloops and yachts. Nearly a quarter century has passed since a "half-crocked, half-nervous" actor and brother-in-law to the American president sought him out at 2:00 A.M. They met in his Laurel Ave. office.

Since talking to Walt Schaefer of the ambulance service, I believe the time of Otash's meeting with Lawford to be extremely significant. It was at about 2:00 A.M. that Schaefer told me his men, "Lieb" and Hunter, picked up Marilyn's body and brought it to the Santa Monica Hospital, where it was eventually removed and returned to her house to be placed, in Sgt. Clemmons's words, "swanlike" on the bed.

Lawford, while speaking to Marilyn after her fight with Bobby, Otash reported, had tried to reason with her. To calm her down, he had urged her to come to the Lawford beach house and relax.

"No, I'm too tired," Marilyn reportedly said. "There is nothing more for me to respond to. Just do me a favor. Tell the president I tried to get him. Tell him goodbye for me. I think my purpose has been served."

CONCLUSION

On Saturday, October 23, 1982, at exactly 2:07 P.M., I closed the file on the Marilyn Conspiracy, case number 72–4813.

Of the more than one million assignments handled by Nick Harris Detectives in its three-quarter-century history, the Marilyn Conspiracy had run the longest. I looked at the massive dossier of correspondence. There were the files on different principals. There was a folder marked "Wrong Door Raid," and a very skimpy volume marked "RTS." There was a stack of photographs, one showing the housekeeper, wearing a benign expression which I knew shielded the great secret of her life. There were the taped conversations, including those with Jack Quinn and Lionel Grandison. I sighed and rang for my secretary. Together we gathered up the bundles and put them on a trolley. We trundled it to a special room.

The Nick Harris investigation into the death of Marilyn Monroe had now reached a new level. The voluminous file was catalogued and entered into the library. In this intimate reading room, with leather chairs and several reading lamps, accessible only to veteran agents, the shelves hold the volumes of completed cases. I joined case file 72–4813, the Marilyn Conspiracy, to a crowded stack with the satisfaction of knowing that between the brand-new, crisp covers of a folder marked "Conclusions and Recommendations," I had answered the chief question: Was Marilyn Monroe murdered? The evidence I gathered in the course of my probe, with the invaluable help of my client, established that there was, indeed, as much justification to classify Marilyn's death as homicide as there was to accept it as a "probable suicide."

Case file 72–4813 also answers the second question: What was Bobby Kennedy's connection with Marilyn's death? My investigation has shown that Bobby Kennedy had dangerous adversaries who shrank at nothing to destroy him. They watched the president's younger brother closely, waiting for the opportunity to pounce on him in a compromising situation. In the final weeks of July 1962, RFK's most deadly enemies, the Hoffa-Giancana group, found in an abandoned sex star grasping at delusions the opportunity to expose Bobby in a bizarre Hollywood love affair that would ruin his political career.

These enemies of the Attorney General used Marilyn Monroe as the means of entrapment, and silenced her as part of their plot.

Marilyn's Monday press conference, which she planned to hold to get even with Bobby "for walking out on her like that," would not only damage RFK's political career, but would also threaten to expose the links among Organized Crime, the White House and the CIA. Thus, by administering a fatal overdose of drugs, Bobby's enemies would be able to achieve their twin objective: Marilyn's death by "overdose" connected to her romance with Bobby would at once politically cripple the Attorney General *and* eliminate at the same time what the mobsters regarded as nothing more than a "dumb blonde," an unreliable "blabbermouth," who was intimate with the affairs of the dangerous men of Cal-Neva.

Without any doubt, my investigation has presented evidence that someone in the Hoffa-Giancana camp was bugging Marilyn's house for the purpose of damaging the Attorney General and the Kennedy family. My report has clearly shown that the bugging of Marilyn's house and telephone calls focused on the Attorney General and was the perfect weapon to demolish the Kennedys' wholesome family image. The surveillance of Marilyn's love affairs with the Kennedys, covering even the "Kennedy-Monroe pillow talk," would give mobsters the chance to blacken that image forever.

That weekend of August 3–5, on the eve of her press conference, and also the weekend when Bobby came to her Brentwood home to say his final goodbye, was an irresistible opportunity for Marilyn's murderers to carry out their plot—entrapping Bobby at the scene of her death. The life of the aging screen star would necessarily be sacrificed to make this scenario possible.

The evidence collected over my thirteen years of studying the Marilyn Conspiracy proves beyond a reasonable doubt the existence of this plot against Marilyn and Bobby.

The activities of wiretappers Spindel and Otash clearly indicate that someone in the Hoffa-Giancana camp was bugging Marilyn's house as part of their counter-offensive against Kennedy, even on the weekend she died. If my client's information and that of many others, including Otash, as well as Lawford's third wife Deborah Gould Lawford, is correct, it is reasonable to assume that Marilyn's killers would know through their electronic surveillance of her, when to move.

To what extent Marilyn knew or perhaps, as suggested by Mrs. Spindel, was an accomplice in attempts to blackmail RFK, is all conjecture. It's a possibility, however, and it should not be excluded from being a motive for someone to silence her. Whoever killed Marilyn, or whoever made off with the red diary, obviously did so to keep Marilyn's sensitive information from reaching public exposure. The importance of neutralizing Marilyn was revealed by the diary entries seen by my client Bob Slatzer. These entries made dangerous reference to Cal-Neva, where one week before her death Marilyn was seen socializing with America's top mobster; according to a 1985 BBC documentary and statements made by Peter Lawford to police, Marilyn Monroe talked at Cal-Neva about her relationship with Bobby Kennedy at a dinner table that included Sam Giancana, then the leading target of Justice Department prosecutions of Organized Crime. Following that probably very unnerving dinner, she apparently went to pieces and, according to Lawford, "overdosed" that evening and was found lying unconscious on the floor of her room at the Cal-Neva Lodge the next morning.

Marilyn's breakup with Bobby Kennedy, in the final weeks of July 1962, came at a time when RFK's adversaries were feeling the greatest pressure from his "Get Hoffa" Squad. They answered by forming their own far more brutal and relentless "Get Bobby Squad," using the body of Marilyn Monroe as their weapon to lure and entrap him. Whoever murdered

Marilyn Monroe did succeed in bringing RFK out in the late afternoon of August 4 to her home on Helena Drive.

There can be no doubt that Marilyn was despondent on the day of her death. Her condition was known to others besides the eavesdroppers. These included her immediate circle: her psychiatrist, Dr. Greenson, her internist, Dr. Engelberg, her housekeeper, her "handler," the hairdresser, the masseur, the lawyer and the handyman—all of whom had knowledge that she was deeply upset about the way she'd been dropped, first by Jack, then by Bobby. A very few knew of Marilyn's abortion which, according to Mike Selsman who worked with Marilyn's public relations girl, Pat Newcomb, took place shortly before her death and whose paternity could have been, according to Marilyn, "either Jack or Bobby."

The depth of Marilyn's despondency was very real. She already had had at least twelve abortions. To have borne a Kennedy child would have been her deepest fantasy come true. Her depression in the last weeks of her life had many causes, some reaching back to the earliest days of Norma Jeane's troubled childhood. Her state of mind was known only to her few friends and confidantes. But it was also known to her enemies—and they would use it to make her death appear to be a suicide, while implicating Bobby Kennedy through his presence at the death scene.

The evidence supports the conclusion that there was more to Marilyn Monroe's death than "probable suicide." The amount of medication found in her body was inconsistent with the physical evidence reported by the Coroner. The high barbiturate levels found in her blood cannot be explained, under the circumstances, by swallowing alone; the fatal dosage must have entered her body by an injection or enema. These facts, along with the glaring inconsistencies contained in the accounts of those who visited Marilyn's house that night, as well as fudged statements given to police by members of Marilyn's entourage, are important enough to establish that an original verdict of a "probable suicide" was either the result of unbelievable negligence or a deliberate cover-up by investigating authorities: the Coroner, the D.A., and the police department.

In order to bring to light what was concealed by the cover-up, one final step remains to be taken: the reopening of the Marilyn Conspiracy investigation.

Although almost all of the known principals in the Marilyn Conspiracy are now dead, the appropriate legal authorities have so far resisted my demand. In order to learn what really happened the night Marilyn died, the remaining eyewitnesses must be heard under oath, which to this day has not been done. While Bob Slatzer and I have taken the findings of this costly and intensive probe to L.A.'s current District Attorney, Ira Reiner, he has demurred, thus, I believe, continuing the cover-up by refusing to recommend that the Grand Jury reopen the investigation. In fact, after being relieved of his post, the foreman of the 1985 Los Angeles Grand Jury publicly called for a new Marilyn investigation and he quickly found himself the target of Reiner's wrath. "The important thing about the affair," the dismissed foreman stated in his departing comments, "is that the name of Marilyn Monroe should be cleared. She's been accused, possibly falsely, of killing herself."

With my hopes of the Grand Jury reopening the

investigation shattered, a last hope offered itself for my findings to be corroborated and brought to public attention by an independent body. This was to have been ABC Television's courageous 1985 Marilyn Monroe investigation for a planned documentary to be shown on the 20/20 news program.

I was first contacted by the 20/20 staff to provide professional consultation, along with Bob Slatzer, in August 1985. According to sources inside ABC, whose confidence I have promised to respect, I can now say for the first time in print that the ABC findings, which were never aired, corroborate my own findings almost one hundred percent. ABC never showed the segment because the network's planned documentary contained such explosive evidence that Kennedy was involved in Marilyn's death, as my client and I had been claiming for years, that ABC's chief executive, Roone Arledge—a close personal friend of RFK's wife Ethel—canceled the show and sent its staff on leave.

According to my sources in ABC, who have intimate knowledge of why the show was canceled, it was the interview with Mrs. Eunice Murray that prompted Arledge to make it seem as if the cover-up was still continuing. The housekeeper, who had maintained for almost twenty-five years that Bobby Kennedy had not visited Marilyn on her death day, stated before ABC's 20/20 Sylvia Chase that RFK had indeed been at Marilyn's house at that very time. This sharp reversal as to RFK's role in the affair after nearly a quarter century of silence by Mrs. Murray supports my own evidence, along with statements recently made by Freddy Otash, that warrant an official and new investigation of this case. To this day, according to Chief Daryl Gates, L.A. Police Department files contain confidential material related to Marilyn's death.

CONCLUSION

I know for certain, however, that the single most important piece of evidence, which literally names her killers, will not be found in police files. The red diary is still missing.

The fate and whereabouts of the red diary are the last remaining mysteries in the conclusion of the Marilyn case. The question is, who took the red diary that night? It first appeared to me that it must have been Marilyn's killer. But I soon became convinced that this conclusion was unlikely; for my client had revealed to me that only three people knew about the diary's existence, Marilyn Monroe, himself, and RFK. Marilyn Monroe told my client weeks before she died how Bobby had reacted to his discovery that she made notes on their conversations. Bobby, Marilyn recalled, had picked up the red diary, and glancing at it a second, flew into a rage, flinging the diary across the room and telling her, "Get rid of this at once."

Based on my client's recollections and the evidence we unearthed, particularly the Otash revelations, I believe that Marilyn's home that night was the target of two operations: one the Giancana-Hoffa "Get Bobby Squad" action to administer her fatal dosage of Nembutal with the object of framing Bobby at Marilyn's death scene; the other, a countermeasure operation organized by the Kennedys *immediately following* Marilyn's death to prevent knowledge of Bobby's involvement from becoming public.

On the basis of statements made by Peter Lawford who organized this "sanitizing" operation at Marilyn's house, coupled with the fact that RFK knew about the red diary's threatening potential, Lawford's operation that night was a daring chance. The risks he took that night were the actions of someone desperately trying to secure the red diary or any other of Marilyn's documents or notes that compromised the Kennedys. According to my sources, recently corroborated by the confessions of "private eye to the stars" Freddy Otash, who served as Peter Lawford's field commander the night Marilyn died, there are still people living at this time who were eyewitnesses to what happened to Marilyn's red diary after she passed away.

My chief concern is the fact that time is running out. There are still important witnesses to the events that became the Marilyn Conspiracy alive today. My investigation has identified these people—even the suspected murderers—to the Los Angeles District Attorney. After thirteen years, my file is closed. The case has been solved to my own satisfaction. Meanwhile, the official version of the causes of the death of Marilyn Monroe continues to remain hidden by a political cover-up.

Mr. E. _. Miller

T. J. Smith

NORMAN MAILER
INFORMATION CONCERNING

To advise of speculation concerning FBI complicity in the death of Marilyn Monroe propounded by author Norman Mailer in his soon-to-be-published biography of the deceased actress.

"Marilyn," a 270-page biography (New York; Grosset and Dunlap,) priced at $19.95, is scheduled for publication on 8/1/73. It reportedly has a first American printing of 285,000 copies and is the August selection of the Book-of-the-Month Club.

Following Miss Monroe's death by drug overdose in 1962, there was a spate of rumors, originating on the West Coast, alleging she was having an affair with the then Attorney General Robert F. Kennedy, and that her death was in some way related to this and/or was the result of a plot revolving around some of her associates who allegedly had past Communist Party affiliations or sympathies. These rumors were embellished upon at that time in various sensational-type gossip magazines and in a short book published in July, 1964, entitled "The Strange Death of Marilyn Monroe" by Frank A. Capell. These allegations were branded false and no factual support existed for them.

Mailer, in his new book, has repeated some of these same rumors and has given them a bizarre twist.

As to whether Miss Monroe took her own life, Mailer answers "possibly" - and then suggests other possibilities. One of these is the suggestion that the FBI, CIA or the Mafia found it of interest that Robert Kennedy, brother of the President John Kennedy, was reputed to be having an affair with the movie star. Mailer suggests that "right-wing" FBI and CIA Agents had a "huge motivation" to murder Marilyn Monroe in order to embarrass the Kennedy family,

1 - 100-370923 (Norman Mailer)
1 - 105-40018 (Marilyn Monroe)

105-40018

NOT RECORDED

152 AUG 1 1973

RPF:rlc
(6)

5 AUG 7 1973

CONTINUED - OVER

FBI report on Norman Mailer, author of first major book to question whether Marilyn committed suicide.

taken an alcoholic beverage or had recently eaten, vomitting

would be possible, but not probable. However, the autopsy dis-

closed that her stomach contained neither alcohol nor food.

OUI ARTICLE: "The finger points to Los Angeles Police Chief William H. PARKER
...He told journalists that the records showed Marilyn had
called Bobby repeatedly during the last week she was alive, making
eight calls to his Justice Department office."

FACTS: During the initial investigation, in 1962, this Department obtained
long distance and toll call records from General Telephone Company.
The records reveal all such calls made from the phones in Miss
MONROE's residence for the period June 1, 1962 through August 18,
1962. Eight calls were reportedly made from her residence to a
Washington D.C. number during this period. Assuming
this was RFK's number, as these were the only calls to Washington
D.C., only one was made within seven days of Marilyn MONROE's
death:

        July 30, 1962 - 8 minutes
        July 23, 1962 - 1 minute
        July 17, 1962 - duration unknown
        July 17, 1962 - duration unknown
        July 16, 1962 - duration unknown
        July 2, 1962 - duration unknown
        July 2, 1962 - duration unknown
        June 25, 1962 - duration unknown

(See Add. 10)

OUI ARTICLE: "It has been reported....that there exists in the vaults of the
Los Angeles Police Department a 723 page report labeled, MARILYN
MONROE-MURDER." CONFIDENTIAL

*Proof of internal police investigation indicating police had
knowledge of RFK's involvement with Marilyn Monroe.*

Coroner's sketch of possible injection site on Marilyn's posterior.

219

Subject: RE-INTERVIEW OF PERSONS KNOWN TO MARILYN MONROE

Date & Time Occurred	Location of Occurrence	Division of Occurrence
August 6, 1962	Various	

Persons, Zones, Assignment, Division		Date & Time Reported
G. H. ARMSTRONG, COMMANDER. WEST L. A. DETECTIVE DIVISION		8-10-62 8:30A

DETAILS

The following is a resume of the interview conducted in an effort to obtain the times of various phone calls received by Miss Monroe on the evening of her death. All of the below times are estimations of the persons interviewed. None are able to state definite times as none checked the time of these calls.

MILTON RUDIN –

Mr. Rudin stated that on the evening of 8-4-62 his exchange received a call at 8:25P and that this call was relayed to him at 8:30P. The call was for him to call Milton Ebbins. At about 8:45P he called Mr. Ebbins who told him that he had received a call from Peter Lawford stating that Mr. Lawford had called Marilyn Monroe at her home and that while Mr. Lawford was talking to her, her voice seemed to "fade out" and when he attempted to call her back, the line was busy. Mr. Ebbins requested that Mr. Rudin call Miss Monroe and determine if everything was alright, or attempt to reach her doctor. At about 9P, Mr. Rudin called Miss Monroe and the phone was answered by Mrs. Murray. He inquired of her as to the physical well being of Miss Monroe and was assured by Mrs. Murray that Miss Monroe was alright. Believing that Miss Monroe was suffering from one of her despondent moments, Mr. Rudin dismissed the possibility of anything further being wrong.

MRS. EUNICE MURRAY –

Mrs. Murray stated that she had worked for Marilyn Monroe since November, 1961, that on the evening of 8-4-62 Miss Monroe had received a collect call from a Joe DiMaggio, Jr. at about 7:30P. Mrs. Murray said that at the time of this call coming in, Miss Monroe was in bed and possibly had been asleep. She took the call and after talking to Joe DiMaggio, Jr., she then made a call to Dr. Greenson and Mrs. Murray overheard her say, "Joe Jr. is not getting married, I'm so happy about this." Mrs. Murray states that from the tone of Miss Monroe's voice, she believed her to be in very good spirits. At about 9P, Mrs. Murray received a call from Mr. Rudin who inquired about Miss Monroe. Mr. Rudin did not talk to Miss Monroe. Mrs. Murray states that these are the only phone calls that she recalls receiving on this date. Note: It is officers opinion that Mrs. Murray was vague and possibly evasive in answering questions pertaining to the activities of Miss Monroe during this time. It is not known whether this is, or is not intentional. During the interrogation of Joe DiMaggio, Jr., he indicated he had made three phone calls to the Monroe home, only one of which Mrs. Murray mentioned.

JOE DiMAGGIO – Miramar Hotel, Room 1035, Santa Monica

Mr. DiMaggio was informed of the rumor which quoted him as saying that

Date & Time Typed	Distribution	Clerk	Employee(s) Reporting	Ser.No.	Div.
8-10-62 9A	WLA	jc	R. E. BYRON	2730	WLA
Supervisor Approving		Serial No. 57	LT. J. H. ARMSTRONG, COMDR	59	WLA

Original police report showing investigator's skepticism of Mrs. Murray's claims.

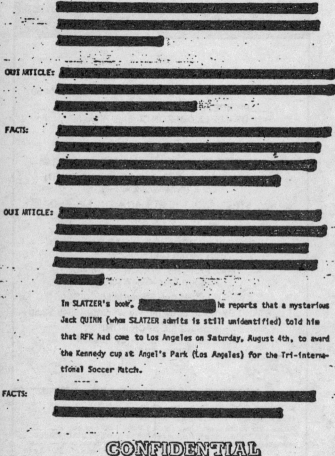

OUI ARTICLE:

FACTS:

OUI ARTICLE:

In SLATZER's book, ▓▓▓▓▓▓▓▓▓ he reports that a mysterious Jack QUINN (whom SLATZER admits is still unidentified) told him that RFK had come to Los Angeles on Saturday, August 4th, to award the Kennedy cup at Angel's Park (Los Angeles) for the Tri-International Soccer Match.

FACTS:

CONFIDENTIAL

For many years police denied having a file on Bob Slatzer. Finally, in 1984, they released this censored portion.